Welcome Entrepreneur

I0398956

This Journal Belongs to:

Current Job:

Location:

HOW TO USE THIS JOURNAL

BECOMING AN ENTREPRENEUR REQUIRES DEDICATION

This journal is intended to be used as a tool to assist you in obtaining the knowledge, organizational skills, and the discipline needed to take your passion or an idea and turn it into a successful brand.

You will benefit from the knowledge, guidance, and expertise that only JAShawPro clients receive when working with me one on one.

Every page of this journal has been handcrafted and tailored specifically to take you and your brand to the next level! The majority of successful business owner have at least one thing in common, we never give up!

As a successful business coach and owner of multiple brands, it is my pleasure to embark on this 6 month journey with you.

Use this journal to create the business of your dreams!

JAShaw.org

SOLID FOUNDATION

ENTREPRENEURSHIP JOURNAL

ENTREPRENEURSHIP

2021 HAS SHOWN US THAT ANYONE CAN OWN A BUSINESS. BUT ENTREPRENEURSHIP ISN'T ABOUT STARTING COMPANIES, IT'S ABOUT HELPING YOURSELF THROUGH HELPING OTHERS.

SOLID FOUNDATION

THIS JOURNAL WAS CREATED TO ASSIST YOU IN THE PLANNING, MARKET RESEARCH, AND DEVELOPMENTAL PHASES OF CREATING A BRAND IN ORDER TO AVOID THE PROCESSES OF REBRANDING, RECONFIGURING, AND STARTING OVER ANEW.

ORGANIZATION

IN ORDER TO BECOME A SUCCESSFUL ENTREPRENEUR, AN ESSENTIAL FIRST STEP IS LEARNING TO BE ORGANIZED. YOUR SOLID FOUNDATION ENTREPRENEUR'S JOURNAL WILL ALLOW YOU TO KEEP EVERYTHING IN ONE PLACE.

DISCIPLINE

ONCE YOU LEARN TO BE METICULOUS ABOUT YOUR BUSINESS AFFAIRS, YOU ARE ABLE TO APPLY A LEVEL OF DISCIPLINE TO YOUR MINDSET THAT WAS UNATTAINABLE BEFORE. WE LIKE TO CALL THIS THE ENTREPRENEUR'S MINDSET.

PROFESSIONALISM

A MAJOR KEY IN NOT ONLY BECOMING BUT MAINTAINING A SUCCESSFUL BUSINESS IS IN YOUR LEVEL OF PROFESSIONALISM. WE WON'T ALLOW YOU TO LET THIS MAJOR ASPECT OF BUSINESS TAKE YOU OUT OF THE GAME.

GETTING TO KNOW THE REAL YOU

WHAT MATTERS MOST TO ME?

WHERE DO I FEEL SAFEST?

WHAT DO I LIKE TO DO FOR FUN?

IF I COULD HAVE ONE WISH, IT WOULD BE?

WHAT IS MY HAPPIEST MEMORY?

WHO ARE MY SUPPORT PEOPLE?

WHAT AM I GRATEFUL FOR?

THE ENTREPRENEURS MINDSET

Living a Disciplined Life is Key to Adopting The Entrepreneurs Mindset

Discipline
/ˈdisəplən/

noun

the practice of training people to obey rules or a code of behavior.

An entrepreneurial mindset is a specific set of beliefs, knowledge, and thought processes that propel entrepreneurial behavior. These codes of behavior enable entrepreneurs to identify and make the most of opportunities, overcome and learn from setbacks, and succeed across multiple areas in life.

In order to achieve this mindset, one must utilize the codes of behavior of the Entrepreneur's mindset:

- Confidence

- Positive Mental Attitude

- Decisiveness

- Creative Mindset

- Self Starting Motivation and Drive

- Accountability

- Ability to Learn from Failure

- Resilience

THE BASICS

BE

- OPEN TO CHANGE
- POSITIVE
- MOTIVATED
- COURAGEOUS
- DETERMINED

EMBRACE

- THE JOURNEY
- UNCOMFORTABILITY
- MISTAKES
- FAILURE
- THE POSSIBILTIES

BEWARE OF

- DOUBT
- FEAR
- JUDGING YOUSELF
- TRYING TO BE PERFECT
- LIMITING BELIEFS

ALWAYS

- KEEP AN OPEN MIND
- DO YOUR RESEARCH
- DOUBLE CHECK YOUR WORK
- EXPECT THE UNEXPECTED
- FOLLOW THROUGH

GETTING TO KNOW THE ENTREPRNEUR IN YOU

WHAT ARE MY STRENGTHS?

WHAT IS MY PROUDEST ACCOMPLISHMENT?

WHAT IS MY BIGGEST FAILURE?

WHAT NEW ACTIVITIES AM I INTERESTED IN OR WILLING TO TRY?

WHAT DO MY DREAMS TELL ME?

WHAT DOES MY INNER CRITIC TELL ME?

IF I WASN'T AFRAID, I WOULD

MY PASSIONS

Write your name in the center circle and things you are
passionate about in the surrounding circles.
When completing this exercise, ask yourself two questions:
What do I want in life?
Who can I help?

When you love what you do, you will work harder
and more passionately than the next person.
This allows you to loose track of time and
never want to stop working instead of dreading work.

MY VALUES

What do I believe in?

POLITICS	RELIGION

SOCIAL ISSUES

VALUES	MORALS

INTEGRITY

COMPLIMENT EXERCISE

Write yourself some compliments- they can focus on both professional and personal traits and skills.

For example, you may express appreciation for your determination to never be late to work or your ability to have uncomfortable conversations with those you love.

....
....
....
....
....
....
....
....
....
....

This exercise allows you to focus on your positive qualities rather than your insecurities. Writing down these compliments enables you to return to them when you feel less confident.

CONFIDENCE BUILDING

Write down the skills you possess in the boxes below.

You can do this exercise alone but I'd also recommend asking family members, friends, and/or coworkers for their insights.

Reflecting on these skills helps
remind us of what makes us special.
Once you identify these skills, you can focus on using and highlighting them throughout your brand to showcase your strengths.

MY SKILLSET

CONFIDENCE STARTER

Pick something off you've always wanted to do
& get started!

Are you passionate about current events?
Start podcasting.
Are you passionate about hustling?
Start selling something.
Are you passionate about stocks?
Start a small investment group.

SOMETHING NEW I TRIED

WHAT WORKED

WHAT DIDN'T WORK

WHAT I LEARNED

CONFIDENCE BUILDING

OVER THE NEXT COUPLE OF WEEKS, KNOCK OUT SOME OF THESE TASKS

TASKS

- [ ] CELEBRATE YOUR WINS
- [ ] DO SOME PUBLIC SPEAKING
- [ ] LET GO OF SMALL MISTAKES
- [ ] CREATE NEW MANTRAS
- [ ] TAKE A RISK
- [ ] ADMIT YOUR FAILURES
- [ ] FIND A SUPPORTIVE MENTOR
- [ ] PROJECT CONFIDENCE
- [ ] ASK FOR ADVICE
- [ ] SMILE MORE

HOW DID I FEEL?

WHAT DID I LEARN?

WHAT DID I GAIN?

For mentoring services please visit JAShaw.org

REJECTION EXERCISE

Rejection is inevitable in the entrepreneurial world.
You'll have friends and family who won't support you,
vendors who won't work with small businesses, stores unwilling
to assist in selling your products, and target audience members
who simply don't want to buy your products.
If you aren't prepared for this, it can devastate your confidence.

It's hard for anyone to get comfortable with rejection,
but the more you face it- the more resilient you'll become.
Try intentionally putting yourself in situations where you know
you'll get rejected and write down your experiences.

....

....

....

....

....

....

....

....

....

....

When you experience rejection and there are no long-term
consequences, you will start to understand how minor
and insignificant most rejections truly are.

POSITIVE MENTAL ATTITUDE

Being positive is something that can be learned.
Becoming an entrepreneur is not for the weak!
The long hours and unstable demands of running
your own business can negatively impact both your
personal life and mental outlook.

One of the easiest ways to cultivate a positive attitude
is to focus on the things you can control. You can control your
diet, amount of sleep and ability to exercise. Each of these
factors will help you stay focused, healthy and positive.

Create a game plan of things you can control
and how you will be better at applying a positive
mental attitude to doing these things.

WHAT I CAN CONTROL

POSITIVE MINDSET EXERCISE

Through the process of meditation,
you are able to control your thoughts and build your confidence.
In a mindfulness practice,
you can learn how to observe your thoughts without judgment.
This clears a blockage allowing you to be able to visualize
yourself accomplishing tasks and being successful.

Over the next couple of days, make time for meditation.

---

5 MINUTE MEDITATION

How did it make you feel?

---

10 MINUTE MEDITATION

How did it make you feel?

---

20 MINUTE MEDITATION

How did it make you feel?

---

30 MINUTE MEDITATION

How did it make you feel?

POSITIVE MINDSET BUILDING

OVER THE NEXT COUPLE OF WEEKS, KNOCK OUT SOME OF THESE TASKS

TASKS

- ☐ AVOID MAKING ASSUMPTIONS
- ☐ GIVE A STRANGER A COMPLIMENT
- ☐ VOLUNTEER OR OFFER HELP
- ☐ STOP NEGATIVE THOUGHTS
- ☐ REFRAIN FROM USING ABSOLUTES
- ☐ INCREASE SOCIAL ACTIVITY
- ☐ MAKE A NEW FRIEND
- ☐ CHANGE UP THE SCENERY
- ☐ HUG SOMEONE
- ☐ NO GOSSIPING

HOW DID I FEEL?

WHAT DID I LEARN?

WHAT DID I GAIN?

DECISIVENESS

The ability to look at a problem or situation,
accurately assess the situation, and make a confident decision
is what it takes to succeed as an entrepreneur.

The ability to make a decision can make or break your future success.
One of the greatest causes of business failure is indecision.
This code of behavior should be practiced and strengthened daily.

Circle your choices below in these
entrepreneurial games of this or that

Products	Services
In Person	Online
Wholesale	Handcrafted
Wix	Shopify
Paid per product/service	Paid per hour

Facebook	Instagram
Videos	Reels
Organic Promo	Paid Promo
Friends&Family	Brand Ambassadors
Creating Content	Hiring Virtual Assistant

Choices

In life, we all have choices.
Based on the passions you listed,
visualize the lifestyle choosing one
of your passions makes for you
and write down what that looks like.

You can either choose to build your brand around this passion
or continue on with your current business idea.

WORST CASE SCENARIO EXERCISE

Fear is the number one thing holding back many entrepreneurs from chasing after their dreams. When you are too afraid to try, you take yourself out the game. This must be faced head on so let's think about the worst case scenario of the passion you chose.

Close your eyes a moment and really, think about it.
Consider what it looks like, how people would look at your failure, how it feels to you, and what you would do about it.
Write down your visualization below

....
....
....
....
....
....
....
....

Did you end up loosing a lot of money and experience a lot of embarrassment? Now tell me, what would happen if these things came to pass? Would you lay down and give up or would you find a path forward?

Once you realize that you can move through a failure,
it is easier to take the next step.

Sacrifices

Now that you have your passion/business idea,
take some time to evaluate the risks associated.
Will you need to take a year off from school,
spend less time with friends, or leave a relationship
in order to meet the demands of the lifestyle you are choosing?

What risks and sacrifices does building an enterprise demand?

When it comes to
building your brand,
there are 3 B's you MUST understand-
Brand, Branding and Brand Identity.

All 3 B's are pieces
of a branding puzzle.
You need all three in order to build
a successful, marketable business.

Without branding, there is no brand.
Without brand identity, there is no branding.

They all build on each other
and you need all three to succeed.

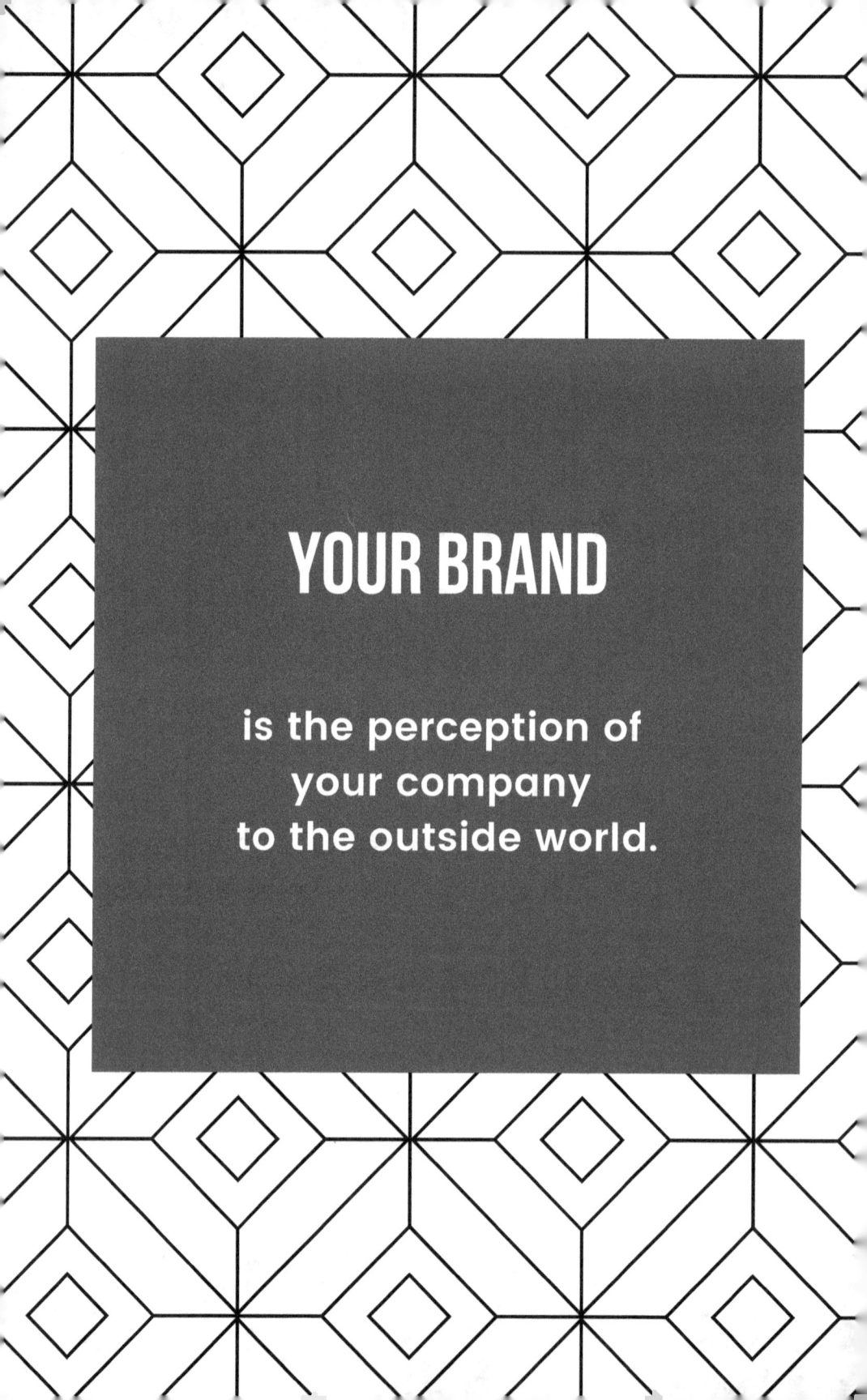

MY BRANDING SPECIFICS

Now that you have your product or service, build on it.
You can list colors that appeal to you, defining words,

What does my brand/business do?

_____

_____

_____

What is my brands niche?

_____

What is my brands personality?

_____

What are my brands values?

_____

What is my brands voice?

_____

Who will my brand/business help?

_____

What will be my brand/business mission?

_____

Who is my brands competition?

_____

BRAND ROLE MODELS

Who are your top 3 brand/business "role models?"

BRAND

WHAT I ADMIRE ABOUT THIS BRAND

BRAND

WHAT I ADMIRE ABOUT THIS BRAND

BRAND

WHAT I ADMIRE ABOUT THIS BRAND

BRANDS WE SEE EVERYDAY

We receive countless emails,
scroll past dozens of ads on social media,
and are bombarded with media marketing on a daily basis.
Take a moment to slow down and really look at
the messaging behind these ads.

How do companies target me?
What colors and designs do they use to appeal?
What part of the message captures my attention?
How does the company deliver their offer?

BRAND OBSERVATION EXERCISE

Gather two products/services you own.
Ask yourself, what emotional connection do I have to these products?
What were the features and benefits that persuaded me
to buy the product/service?

PRODUCT/SERVICE

EMOTIONAL CONNECTION

FEATURES/BENEFITS

PRODUCT/SERVICE

EMOTIONAL CONNECTION

FEATURES/BENEFITS

BRAND STRATEGY EXERCISE

With your product/service in mind-
What emotional connection, features, and benefits
would you like customers to experience with your product?

PRODUCT/SERVICE

EMOTIONAL CONNECTION

FEATURES/BENEFITS

This exercise helps you identify the type of emotional connection
you want to have with your customers as well as
features and benefits you want to highlight.

MY BRANDS WHY

People don't buy what you do,
they buy why you do it.

Why do you provide this service or
Why do you sell this product?

....

....

....

....

....

....

....

....

....

....

....

Why you do what you do, the way you do it-
is what sets you apart!

Your why becomes the purpose behind your brand/business
and that provides you with motivation.

MY BRAND'S NAME

A brand name is a Trademark.
Your brands name can alter the perception and reality of
how the world perceives your brand versus the competition.

DOES YOUR BRAND/BUSINES NAME HAVE ANY NEGATIVE CONNOTATIONS?

IS YOUR BRAND/BUSINESS NAME EASY TO SAY AND READ?

CAN YOUR BRAND/BUSINESS NAME GROW WITH YOU?

IS YOUR BRAND/BUSINESS NAME AVAILABLE TO BE TRADEMARKED?

IS YOUR BRAND/BUSINESS NAME AVAILABLE ACROSS VARIOUS SOCIAL MEDIA PLATFORMS?

IS YOUR BRAND/BUSINESS NAME AVAILABLE TO BE USED AS A DOMAIN NAME?

WHAT IS YOUR BRAND/BUSINESS NAME?

MY BRAND'S STORY

Every brand has a story and your brand story is another factor that sets you apart from the competition. Your brand story should include your history- how and why you were founded as well as the role your brand plays in your customer's life.

How do you make your customer a hero? It is through making them more relaxed in their day to day operations so they are able to be more productive. Or does your product assist them in fixing their credit in order for them to purchase their first home.

....

....

....

....

....

....

....

....

....

....

....

This story is an important basis for your
brand identity and marketing content.

TARGET AUDIENCE PERSONA

Imagine your brand/business has an average customer- who is he or she, how does he or she spend their time, where does he or she shop?

NAME

OCCUPATION

AGE

RELATIONSHIP STATUS

SEX

KIDS

LOCATION

INCOME

HOBBIES

FAVORITE BRANDS/BUSINESSES

VALUES

ASPIRATIONS

OBSTACLES

MY BRAND'S COLORS

Colors are associated with emotions.
Your brand's primary and supporting colors are
an important piece of your brand identity.
When you select colors that are representative of your brand values,
you can immediately communicate your brand's mission.

BLUE: INTEGRITY, CALM, TRUST, TRANQUILITY, LOYALTY, DEPENDABILITY, INTELLIGENCE
GREEN: WEALTH, GROWTH, FRESHNESS, ENVIRONMENTAL-FRIENDLINESS, NATURE
YELLOW: HAPPINESS, ORIGINALITY, ENERGY, POSITIVITY
PURPLE: ROYALTY, SPIRITUALITY, LUXURY, QUALITY
PINK: FEMININITY, COMPASSION, PLAYFULNESS
RED: POWERFUL, STRONG/STRENGTH, PASSION
ORANGE: COURAGE, ORIGINALITY, SUCCESS, BOLD, FUN
WHITE: CLEANLINESS, PURITY, FRESHNESS, INNOCENCE
BLACK: ELEGANCE, DRAMA, STRENGTH, SOPHISTICATED, SECURITY

WHAT PRIMARY COLOR DO I CHOOSE TO REPRESENT MY BRAND AND WHY?

WHAT SECONDARY COLORS DO I CHOOSE TO REPRESENT MY BRAND AND WHY?

DOES MY BRAND'S VALUES AND MISSION COME ACROSS IN MY COLOR CHOICES?

MY BRAND'S FONTS

Typography refers to the certain fonts you utilize throughout your brand. It can evoke feelings of energy, authority, elegance, traditionalism and more. Similar to colors, fonts are associated with emotions and adjectives.

SERIF FONTS- TIMES NEW ROMAN, GEORGIA, AND GARAMOND
REPRESENTATIVE OF: AUTHORITY, TRADITION, RESPECT

SANS SERIF FONTS- HELVETICA, ARIAL, AND VERDANA
REPRESENTATIVE OF: MODERN, CLEAN, STABLE

SLAB SERIF FONTS- ROCKWELL, COURIER, AND MUSEO
REPRESENTATIVE OF: BOLD, STRONG, MODERN

SCRIPT FONTS-LOBSTER, LUCIDA, AND BRUSH SCRIPT
REPRESENTATIVE OF: ELEGANCE, LUXURY, CREATIVE

MODERN FONTS- POLITICA, EUROSTYLE, AND MATCHBOOK
REPRESENTATIVE OF: BOLD, FASHIONABLE, STYLISH, EXCLUSIVE

MY BRAND'S FONTS

Pro tip: Remember all fonts are not free. You can use fonts on Canva if you have a paid subscription. Otherwise, look up the font name you choose in order to obtain a license for use.

MY BRANDS LOGO

Brainstorm how you'd like your brand's logo to look

While designing your brand/business logo,
answer the following questions-
Does it make an impression? Stand out in a visually appealing way? Clearly communicate who you are? Stand the test of time?

MY BRAND KIT
Finalize your branding here

Primary Logo

Color Palette

Hex Codes

Secondary Logo

Alternative Logo

Fav Icon

Typography

Hashtags

WEBSITE HOSTING

Check out the top hosting options available

GoDaddy

Pros: One stop shop, easy to use, moderately priced, good website capability

Cons: Limited design capability and bad customer service

Shopify

Pros: Popular, easy to use, moderately priced

Cons: Only an online store- not a full website, extremely limited design capability

Big Cartel

Pros: Popular, easy to use, moderately priced

Cons: Only an online store- not a full website, extremely limited design capability

Wordpress

Pros: Easy to use, free version available

Cons: Limited customer service, limited design capability, limited website capability, outdated website builder, expensive unless used with a third party for ex: godaddy

Wix

Pros: Easy to use, full website capability, good design capability, great customer service, free version available- highly recommended by JAShawPro

Cons: Can be pricey, slight learning curve

LANDING PAGES

Not yet ready for a website but need an online presence

What is a landing page?

A landing page is a web pages where there
is only one action to take.
The more buttons and links you place on a
web page, the more likely they are to be distracted.

Why would I need a landing page?

If you are not yet ready for a full website or it is
simply not in this month's budget, a landing page
will encourage users to take an action,
such as joining your list or buying your products.

How much does a landing page cost?

You can build a free landing page through your
hosting provider. Or if you don't have a hosting
provider yet, there are other services that allow
you to create free landing pages.

Who should I go through for my landing page?

I highly recommend using Mailchimp.
Sidenote: design capability on Mailchimp is limited.
The service is free & the purpose of a landing page
is normally to inform or get subscribers so this page
doesn't need to be highly decorative.

MARKETING YOUR BRAND

is the efforts your company makes (ex: social media, e marketing, networking, direct marketing, etc.) with the goal of reaching your target audience to communicate the benefits of your product or service.

CHOOSING SOCIAL NETWORKS

FACEBOOK

- 1.79 billion daily users worldwide Audience: Generation X and millennials
- Industry impact: B2C
- Best for: Brand awareness; advertising

INSTAGRAM

- 1 billion monthly users
- Audience: Primarily millennials
- Industry impact: B2C
- Best for: Natural-looking media, behind-the-scenes, and user-generated content; advertising

TWITTER

- 186 mil daily users worldwide
- Audience: Primarily millennials Industry impact: B2B and B2C
- Best for: Public relations; customer service

PINTEREST

- 416 mil monthly users worldwide
- Audience: Primarily older millennials and younger baby boomers
- Industry impact: B2C
- Best for: Visual advertising; inspiration

LINKEDIN

- 675 mil monthly users worldwide
- Audience: Baby boomers, Generation X, and millennials
- Industry impact: B2B
- Best for: B2B relationships, business development, and employment marketing

SOCIAL MEDIA STRATEGY EXERCISE

Choose the best three networks you'd like to
explore in promoting your brand and state why
you chose to use these platforms.

NETWORK 1

NETWORK 2

NETWORK 3

After our first 6 months,
I challenge you to come back and reevaluate
if these networks are working for your brand.

CREATING CONTENT

IMAGE SIZING

 1080 x 1080px

 1200 x 1200 px

 1024 x 1024px

GRAPHIC DESIGN

- Canva
- illustrator
- Photoshop
- PicMonkey

ANALYTICS

- Google Analytics
- Iconosquare
- Pintrest
- Twitter

POST SCHEDULING

- Facebook
- Buffer
- Later
- Hootsuite

DAILY MAINTENANCE

- Create content
- Engage with following

WEEKLY MAINTENANCE

- Check your analytics
- Engage with partners

MONTHLY MAINTENANCE

- Plan monthly posts
- Social media audit

If you need assistance with content creation, please visit jashawpro.org

BUILDING AN EMAIL LIST

E marketing is one of the oldest but most effective digital marketing channels

Quality Versus Quantity

The goal is to secure complete information from real people.

Similar to followers, don't buy an email list!
Bots, spam accounts, and abandoned email addresses don't make purchases.

You cannot use a gmail, yahoo, etc. email address to do email marketing.
A business email address must be purchased.

Email Service Providers

MailChimp and ConvertKit are free up to a certain number of subscribers.

Wix also offers an in house e marketing system through ascend.

How to set up

Through your email service provider or website builder, you will set up a form to capture the visitors email address and any other pertinent information. The form can either be embedded directly onto your website, landing page, or pop up.

If you need assistance with content creation, please visit jashawpro.org

BRAND READINESS CHECKLIST

Before announcing your brand to the world, complete these items

- [ ] Finalize logo draft
- [ ] Trademark your brand name
- [ ] Purchase domain name
- [ ] Create social networks with your brand name
- [ ] Purchase a business email address
- [ ] Create social media headers
- [ ] Get business cards made for your brand
- [ ] Create a social media launch advertisement
- [ ] Create a landing page to capture subscribers

If you need assistance with any of these items, please visit jashawpro.org for starter packages

NETWORKING EXERCISE

One of the most valuable skills an entrepreneur can learn to make their company a success is networking. It takes time, energy, dedication, and more to create a successful brand. It's of most importance to have built a community of like minded individuals to draw energy from and keep you motivated. When networking, you are able to extend your skills, learn from others success, get new customers, and tell others about your brand.

Task: Find a few local networking events in your area.
Tip: You should have business cards on hand, your social media accounts set up, landing page or website, and email list ready for others to subscribe. Come back and write down your experiences.

....
....
....
....
....
....
....
....
....
....

In order to get your brand off the ground,
you must come from behind the computer screen.

ELEVATOR PITCH EXERCISE

Every entrepreneur needs to perfect an elevator pitch.
Writing yours can give you more confidence
when it comes to speaking for your brand.

Your pitch should describe your business model to someone
who's never heard of it before. It's called an elevator pitch because
you should be able to deliver it in the time it takes for an elevator to
get to your floor — give or take 30 seconds.
It's going to take time to identify and polish the most
important pieces of information to deliver during this pitch,
and you'll need to practice it multiple times to get the delivery right.

....
....
....
....
....
....
....
....
....
....

When you do get it right,
you'll feel more confident talking to others about your brand.

FEEDBACK

After a substantial amount of practice,
go out and deliver your elevator pitch to 5 people.
Pay attention to their body language and make a note
when the person "lit up" or "got it" — that's valuable information.
Also, notice when someone is confused and asks questions.
What questions did they ask, where did they need clarification?
Then incorporate that into your message.

Come back and jot down your experience and their reaction.

....
....
....
....
....
....
....
....
....
....

You'll need to do this multiple times before you have all the
right piece of information and can deliver it flawlessly.
Keep at it!

PROFESSIONALISM

Professionalism is a set of values/morals
that affects the way you dress, speak, behave, and
make decisions in all situations related to your brand/business.

Communication
As an entrepreneur, it is of utmost importance for you to keep your word which includes communicating with others when you have promised to do so and always meeting deadlines- even missing social events and loosing sleep to do so. When you choose to make a commitment, because it is a choice, you need to honor it.

Demeanor
As an entrepreneur, you will experience undo stress and constant setbacks on your journey to success. Your ability to remain composed through the hardest of circumstances will make all the difference.
You will make better decision because of it.

Reputation
Word of Mouth is everything when it comes to getting your brand started and maintaining a good reputation. Your reputation is solidified through your brands high level of integrity throughout every aspect of your business. Your customer service skills will make or break the success of your brand.

Accountability
As an entrepreneur, you will make mistakes. It's okay, everyone does it. It is what happens after you make a mistake that makes all the difference. It is important to acknowledge you mistake, apologize for the error, amend the situation, and learn from the situation so it doesn't happen again.

CUSTOMER SERVICE

Remember that the customer experience begins as soon as the customer hears about your business.

Making a good first impression will always set the tone!

Treat your customers as individuals (sometimes you'll need to make am exception to keep the customer.)

Listen to your customers, provide personalized service and make it about them, not you!

TIME MANAGEMENT

Free yourself from unnecessary tasks and obligations. A big part of time management is saying "no" when necessary. This also includes preparing agendas for meetings to keep them concise, arrive on time for appointments, and giving up multitasking in favor of fully focusing on tasks one by one.

TIME AUDIT

How do I spend my time?

Take some time to break down the last three days
and how you spent your time. This exercise gives you insight
on whether your current actions are matching up with your goals.

Are you actively working towards your goals?

....
....
....
....
....
....
....
....
....
....
....
....

Evaluating where your time goes starts a process of realigning
your actions and choices with what's really important to you.

TIME MANAGEMENT

LEARN TO AVOID — URGENT & NOT IMPORTANT
- Interruptions
- Some Meetings and Calls
- Busy Work

LEARN TO MANAGE — URGENT & IMPORTANT
- Crises
- Deadline-Driven Tasks
- Things That Need Immediate Attention/Action

LEARN TO LIMIT — NOT IMPORTANT & NOT URGENT
- Wasting Time
- Entertainment
- Self Doubt

LEARN TO FOCUS — NOT URGENT & IMPORTANT
- Planning & Finding New Opportunities
- Relationship Building
- Personal Growth

ACCOUNTABILITY

Everything that happens to your business – you are responsible for.

From this moment forward, you must accept responsibility for everything in your life and hold yourself accountable to it.

BUSINESS GOALS

Choose five business goals to focus on for the next six months.

JASHAWPRO

MY RESILIENCE PLAN

People I can call or talk to for help:
- _____
- _____
- _____

How I can look after myself:
_____
_____
_____
_____

My motivation:
1. _____
2. _____
3. _____

What has helped me in the past:
_____
_____
_____
_____
_____
_____

Advice I would give a friend:
_____
_____
_____
_____
_____
_____

M	T	W	T	F	S	S

Top Priorities

_____
_____
_____
_____
_____
_____
_____
_____
_____
_____

Notes

MONTHLY GOALS

MY FOCUS IS ON	MILESTONES
	1
	2
	3

DO	DON'T	MAIN GOALS
		1
		2
		3
		4
		5

IMPORTANT DATES

GOAL SUGGESTIONS

REACH OUT TO AN INFLUENCER	HEALTHY WORK/LIFE BALANCE	PRACTICE CONFIDENCE	EMAIL 10 NEW PROSPECTS ABOUT MY BUSINESS	LET GO OF LIMITING BELIEFS	IMPROVE CUSTOMER ENGAGEMENT
WORK ON MY SOCIAL MEDIA PRESENCE	PRACTICE DECISVENESS	LEARN A NEW SKILL	INCREASE SALES	PRACTICE MINDFULNESS	REDUCE BUSINESS EXPENSES
FIND NEW HOBBIES	WORK ON MY MARKETING STRATEGY	DELEGATE EFFECTIVELY	STAND UP TO MY FEARS	WORK WITH IDEAL CLIENTS	PLAN MY MARKETING CALENDAR

MONTHLY BUDGET

MONTH OF: _____

INCOME			
DATE	SOURCE	CATEGORY	AMOUNT

BILLS & FIXED EXPENSES		
DATE	SOURCE	AMOUNT

VARIABLE EXPENSES		
DATE	SOURCE	AMOUNT

SUMMARY	
SOURCE	AMOUNT
INCOME	
BILLS & FIXED EXPENSES	
VARIABLE EXPENSES	
BALANCE	

SOCIAL MEDIA POSTING SCHEDULE

Test out the three social media networks you chose to focus on

Month: _____ **Monthly Focus:** _____

NETWORK	SUN	MON	TUE	WED	THU	FRI	SAT

NETWORK	SUN	MON	TUE	WED	THU	FRI	SAT

NETWORK	SUN	MON	TUE	WED	THU	FRI	SAT

NETWORK	SUN	MON	TUE	WED	THU	FRI	SAT

PROGRESS TRACKER

START BY COLORING IN EACH BOX IN THE GRAY KEY AREA WITH A DIFFERENT COLOR. NEXT TO THE BOX, YOU WILL CREATE PERFORMANCE METRICS FOR THE MONTH.
FOR EX: PROJECTS COMPLETED, NEW CLIENTS, RETURNING CLIENTS, SOCIAL MEDIA GROWTH, SALES, WEBSITE SUBSCRIBERS, ETC.

WHENEVER YOU MAKE PROGRESS THIS MONTH TOWARDS ONE OF THESE GOALS, COME BACK AND FILL IN A PART OF THE WOLF WITH THE CORRESPONDING COLOR.

DAILY GRATITUDE LOG

WRITE DOWN 3 THINGS YOU ARE GRATEFUL FOR ON EACH LINE

1. ....
2. ....
3. ....
4. ....
5. ....
6. ....
7. ....
8. ....
9. ....
10. ....
11. ....
12. ....
13. ....
14. ....
15. ....
16. ....
17. ....
18. ....
19. ....
20. ....
21. ....
22. ....
23. ....
24. ....
25. ....
26. ....
27. ....
28. ....
29. ....
30. ....
31. ....

WEEKLY GOALS

- ✗ ....
- ✗ ....
- ✗ ....
- ✗ ....
- ✗ ....
- ✗ ....
- ✗ ....

WEEK SPECIFIC BOUNDARIES

I AM _____
(INSERT AFFIRMATION ABOVE)

This week, I Will Challenge Myself To:	Mon	Tues	Weds	Thurs	Fri

Weekly Tasks

MON TUE WED THU FRI

FOR THE
WEEK OF:

RISING RITUAL

I Will Raise My Vibration By: Mon   Tues   Wed   Thurs   Fri

_____

_____

_____

_____

_____

RITUAL SUGGESTIONS

EARLY RISE/ EARLY SET	GO TECH FREE	PRIORITIZE BALANCE	RECITE MY AFFIRMATIONS	JOURNAL
GO FOR A WALK	MORNING/ EVENING DRINK	SET MILESTONES	BREATHWORK	VISUALIZE SUCCESS
READ	TAKE A HERBAL BATH	EXPRESS GRATITUDE	CLEAN UP	PAMPER MYSELF
UNPLUG	REVIEW GOALS & TO-DO LISTS	WORK DELIBERATELY	SET INTENTIONS	EMBRACE NATURE
FEED MY MIND	EXERCISE	MEDITATE	GET ORGANIZED	LISTEN TO A PODCAST

DON'T OVER STRESS YOURSELF TO AVOID FATIGUE. IT'S NEARLY IMPOSSIBLE TO BE IN A POSITIVE MENTAL STATE WHEN YOUR BODY IS STRESSED OUT.

WEEKLY EXERCISE
THIS WEEK I CHOOSE TO...

- _____
- _____
- _____
- _____
- _____
- _____

WEEKLY FOOD DIARY
LESS OR MORE OF WHAT?

Breakfast:

Lunch:

Dinner:

Snacks:

Beverages:

FITNESS SUGGESTIONS

Do Yoga	Martial Arts	Go for a Walk	Take the Stairs	Eat Less Meat
No sugar	Go Swimming	Dance Party	Team Sports	Yard Work
Do Pilates	Jump Rope	Spin Class	Go Skating	Do Squats
Meat Less Monday	Tae Kwon Do	Do Zumba	Do Tai Chi	Kick Boxing
Ride a Bike	Water Fast	Less Carbs	Go Hiking	Do Cardio

EVENING RITUAL

I Will Maintain My Vibration By:	Mon	Tues	Wed	Thurs	Fri
_____	○	○	○	○	○
_____	○	○	○	○	○
_____	○	○	○	○	○
_____	○	○	○	○	○
_____	○	○	○	○	○
_____	○	○	○	○	○

RITUAL SUGGESTIONS LOCATED ON THE RISING RITUALS PAGE

SLEEP CHECK

Getting enough sleep daily ensures you are well rested and ready to tackle the day. Try pushing for seven to eight hours of sleep a night

	SUN	MON	TUE	WED	THU	FRI	SAT
Go to sleep time							
Wake up time							
How long I slept							

WEEKLY REFLECTION

GOALS ACHIEVED:

HIGHLIGHTS:

GOALS FOR NEXT WEEK:

WEEKEND RESTORATION
ADD YOUR WEEKEND SELF CARE PLANS BELOW

-
-
-

WEEKLY GOALS

- ✗ ....
- ✗ ....
- ✗ ....
- ✗ ....
- ✗ ....
- ✗ ....
- ✗ ....

WEEK SPECIFIC BOUNDARIES

I AM _____
(INSERT AFFIRMATION ABOVE)

This week, I Will Challenge Myself To:	Mon	Tues	Weds	Thurs	Fri

Weekly Tasks

MON
TUE
WED
THU
FRI

FOR THE
WEEK OF:

RISING RITUAL

I Will Raise My Vibration By:

	Mon	Tues	Wed	Thurs	Fri
_____	○	○	○	○	○
_____	○	○	○	○	○
_____	○	○	○	○	○
_____	○	○	○	○	○
_____	○	○	○	○	○

RITUAL SUGGESTIONS

EARLY RISE/ EARLY SET	GO TECH FREE	PRIORITIZE BALANCE	RECITE YOUR AFFIRMATIONS	JOURNAL
GO FOR A WALK	MORNING/ EVENING DRINK	SET MILESTONES	BREATHWORK	VISUALIZE SUCCESS
READ	TAKE A HERBAL BATH	EXPRESS GRATITUDE	CLEAN UP	PAMPER YOURSELF
UNPLUG	REVIEW GOALS & TO-DO LISTS	WORK DELIBERATELY	SET INTENTIONS	EMBRACE NATURE
FEED YOUR MIND	EXERCISE	MEDITATE	GET ORGANIZED	LISTEN TO A PODCAST

DON'T OVER STRESS YOURSELF TO AVOID FATIGUE. IT'S NEARLY IMPOSSIBLE TO BE IN A POSITIVE MENTAL STATE WHEN YOUR BODY IS STRESSED OUT.

WEEKLY EXERCISE
THIS WEEK I CHOOSE TO...

- _____
- _____
- _____
- _____
- _____
- _____

WEEKLY FOOD DIARY
LESS OR MORE OF WHAT?

Breakfast: _____

Lunch: _____

Dinner: _____

Snacks: _____

Beverages: _____

FITNESS SUGGESTIONS

Do Yoga	Martial Arts	Go for a Walk	Take the Stairs	Eat Less Meat
No sugar	Go Swimming	Dance Party	Team Sports	Yard Work
Do Pilates	Jump Rope	Spin Class	Go Skating	Do Squats
Meat Less Monday	Tae Kwon Do	Do Zumba	Do Tai Chi	Kick Boxing
Ride a Bike	Water Fast	Less Carbs	Go Hiking	Do Cardio

EVENING RITUAL

I Will Maintain My Vibration By:	Mon	Tues	Wed	Thurs	Fri
_____	○	○	○	○	○
_____	○	○	○	○	○
_____	○	○	○	○	○
_____	○	○	○	○	○
_____	○	○	○	○	○
_____	○	○	○	○	○

RITUAL SUGGESTIONS LOCATED ON THE RISING RITUALS PAGE

SLEEP CHECK

Getting enough sleep daily ensures you are well rested and ready to tackle the day. Try pushing for seven to eight hours of sleep a night

	SUN	MON	TUE	WED	THU	FRI	SAT
Go to sleep time							
Wake up time							
How long I slept							

WEEKLY REFLECTION

GOALS ACHIEVED:

HIGHLIGHTS:

GOALS FOR NEXT WEEK:

WEEKEND RESTORATION
ADD YOUR WEEKEND SELF CARE PLANS BELOW

-
-
-

WEEKLY GOALS

- ✗ ....
- ✗ ....
- ✗ ....
- ✗ ....
- ✗ ....
- ✗ ....
- ✗ ....

WEEK SPECIFIC BOUNDARIES

I AM _____
(INSERT AFFIRMATION ABOVE)

This week, I Will Challenge Myself To:

	Mon	Tues	Weds	Thurs	Fri

Weekly Tasks

MON TUE WED THU FRI

FOR THE WEEK OF:

RISING RITUAL

I Will Raise My Vibration By:

	Mon	Tues	Wed	Thurs	Fri
_____	○	○	○	○	○
_____	○	○	○	○	○
_____	○	○	○	○	○
_____	○	○	○	○	○
_____	○	○	○	○	○

RITUAL SUGGESTIONS

EARLY RISE / EARLY SET	GO TECH FREE	PRIORITIZE BALANCE	RECITE YOUR AFFIRMATIONS	JOURNAL
GO FOR A WALK	MORNING / EVENING DRINK	SET MILESTONES	BREATHWORK	VISUALIZE SUCCESS
READ	TAKE A HERBAL BATH	EXPRESS GRATITUDE	CLEAN UP	PAMPER YOURSELF
UNPLUG	REVIEW GOALS & TO-DO LISTS	WORK DELIBERATELY	SET INTENTIONS	EMBRACE NATURE
FEED YOUR MIND	EXERCISE	MEDITATE	GET ORGANIZED	LISTEN TO A PODCAST

DON'T OVER STRESS YOURSELF TO AVOID FATIGUE. IT'S NEARLY IMPOSSIBLE TO BE IN A POSITIVE MENTAL STATE WHEN YOUR BODY IS STRESSED OUT.

WEEKLY EXERCISE
THIS WEEK I CHOOSE TO...

- _____
- _____
- _____
- _____
- _____
- _____

WEEKLY FOOD DIARY
LESS OR MORE OF WHAT?

Breakfast:

Lunch:

Dinner:

Snacks:

Beverages:

FITNESS SUGGESTIONS

Do Yoga	Martial Arts	Go for a Walk	Take the Stairs	Eat Less Meat
No sugar	Go Swimming	Dance Party	Team Sports	Yard Work
Do Pilates	Jump Rope	Spin Class	Go Skating	Do Squats
Meat Less Monday	Tae Kwon Do	Do Zumba	Do Tai Chi	Kick Boxing
Ride a Bike	Water Fast	Less Carbs	Go Hiking	Do Cardio

EVENING RITUAL

I Will Maintain My Vibration By:

	Mon	Tues	Wed	Thurs	Fri
_____	○	○	○	○	○
_____	○	○	○	○	○
_____	○	○	○	○	○
_____	○	○	○	○	○
_____	○	○	○	○	○
_____	○	○	○	○	○

RITUAL SUGGESTIONS LOCATED ON THE RISING RITUALS PAGE

SLEEP CHECK

Getting enough sleep daily ensures you are well rested and ready to tackle the day. Try pushing for seven to eight hours of sleep a night

	SUN	MON	TUE	WED	THU	FRI	SAT
Go to sleep time							
Wake up time							
How long I slept							

WEEKLY REFLECTION

GOALS ACHIEVED:

HIGHLIGHTS:

GOALS FOR NEXT WEEK:

WEEKEND RESTORATION

ADD YOUR WEEKEND SELF CARE PLANS BELOW

WEEKLY GOALS

✗ ....
✗ ....
✗ ....
✗ ....
✗ ....
✗ ....
✗ ....

WEEK SPECIFIC BOUNDARIES

I AM _____
(INSERT AFFIRMATION ABOVE)

This week, I Will Challenge Myself To:

	Mon	Tues	Weds	Thurs	Fri

Weekly Tasks

MON
TUE
WED
THU
FRI

FOR THE
WEEK OF:

RISING RITUAL

I Will Raise My Vibration By:

	Mon	Tues	Wed	Thurs	Fri
_____	○	○	○	○	○
_____	○	○	○	○	○
_____	○	○	○	○	○
_____	○	○	○	○	○
_____	○	○	○	○	○

RITUAL SUGGESTIONS

EARLY RISE/ EARLY SET	GO TECH FREE	PRIORITIZE BALANCE	RECITE YOUR AFFIRMATIONS	JOURNAL
GO FOR A WALK	MORNING/ EVENING DRINK	SET MILESTONES	BREATHWORK	VISUALIZE SUCCESS
READ	TAKE A HERBAL BATH	EXPRESS GRATITUDE	CLEAN UP	PAMPER YOURSELF
UNPLUG	REVIEW GOALS & TO-DO LISTS	WORK DELIBERATELY	SET INTENTIONS	EMBRACE NATURE
FEED YOUR MIND	EXERCISE	MEDITATE	GET ORGANIZED	LISTEN TO A PODCAST

DON'T OVER STRESS YOURSELF TO AVOID FATIGUE. IT'S NEARLY IMPOSSIBLE TO BE IN A POSITIVE MENTAL STATE WHEN YOUR BODY IS STRESSED OUT.

WEEKLY EXERCISE
THIS WEEK I CHOOSE TO...

- _____
- _____
- _____
- _____
- _____
- _____

WEEKLY FOOD DIARY
LESS OR MORE OF WHAT?

Breakfast:

Lunch:

Dinner:

Snacks:

Beverages:

FITNESS SUGGESTIONS

Do Yoga	Martial Arts	Go for a Walk	Take the Stairs	Eat Less Meat
No sugar	Go Swimming	Dance Party	Team Sports	Yard Work
Do Pilates	Jump Rope	Spin Class	Go Skating	Do Squats
Meat Less Monday	Tae Kwon Do	Do Zumba	Do Tai Chi	Kick Boxing
Ride a Bike	Water Fast	Less Carbs	Go Hiking	Do Cardio

EVENING RITUAL

I Will Maintain My Vibration By: Mon   Tues   Wed   Thurs   Fri

_____

_____

_____

_____

_____

_____

RITUAL SUGGESTIONS LOCATED ON THE RISING RITUALS PAGE

SLEEP CHECK

Getting enough sleep daily ensures you are well rested and ready to tackle the day. Try pushing for seven to eight hours of sleep a night

	SUN	MON	TUE	WED	THU	FRI	SAT
Go to sleep time							
Wake up time							
How long I slept							

WEEKLY REFLECTION

GOALS ACHIEVED:

HIGHLIGHTS:

GOALS FOR NEXT WEEK:

WEEKEND RESTORATION
ADD YOUR WEEKEND SELF CARE PLANS BELOW

END OF MONTH RECAP

SMALL WINS
1. _____
2. _____
3. _____

BIG ACHIEVEMENTS
1. _____
2. _____
3. _____

HIGHLIGHTS

LESSONS I LEARNED

WHAT WORKED

WHAT I'LL STOP DOING

IMPROVEMENTS TO MAKE

M	T	W	T	F	S	S

Top Priorities

_____
_____
_____
_____
_____
_____
_____
_____
_____

Notes

MONTHLY GOALS

MY FOCUS IS ON

MILESTONES
1
2
3

DO   DON'T

MAIN GOALS
1
2
3
4
5

IMPORTANT DATES

GOAL SUGGESTIONS

REACH OUT TO AN INFLUENCER	HEALTHY WORK/LIFE BALANCE	PRACTICE CONFIDENCE	EMAIL 10 NEW PROSPECTS ABOUT MY BUSINESS	LET GO OF LIMITING BELIEFS	IMPROVE CUSTOMER ENGAGEMENT
WORK ON MY SOCIAL MEDIA PRESENCE	PRACTICE DECISVENESS	LEARN A NEW SKILL	INCREASE SALES	PRACTICE MINDFULNESS	REDUCE BUSINESS EXPENSES
FIND NEW HOBBIES	WORK ON MY MARKETING STRATEGY	DELEGATE EFFECTIVELY	STAND UP TO MY FEARS	WORK WITH IDEAL CLIENTS	PLAN MY MARKETING CALENDAR

MONTHLY BUDGET

MONTH OF: _____

INCOME

DATE	SOURCE	CATEGORY	AMOUNT

BILLS & FIXED EXPENSES

DATE	SOURCE	AMOUNT

VARIABLE EXPENSES

DATE	SOURCE	AMOUNT

SUMMARY

SOURCE	AMOUNT
INCOME	
BILLS & FIXED EXPENSES	
VARIABLE EXPENSES	
BALANCE	

SOCIAL MEDIA POSTING SCHEDULE

Test out the three social media networks you chose to focus on

Month: _____ **Monthly Focus:** _____

NETWORK	SUN	MON	TUE	WED	THU	FRI	SAT

NETWORK	SUN	MON	TUE	WED	THU	FRI	SAT

NETWORK	SUN	MON	TUE	WED	THU	FRI	SAT

NETWORK	SUN	MON	TUE	WED	THU	FRI	SAT

PROGRESS TRACKER

KEY

START BY COLORING IN EACH BOX IN THE GRAY KEY AREA WITH A DIFFERENT COLOR. NEXT TO THE BOX, YOU WILL CREATE PERFORMANCE METRICS FOR THE MONTH.
FOR EX: PROJECTS COMPLETED, NEW CLIENTS, RETURNING CLIENTS, SOCIAL MEDIA GROWTH, SALES, WEBSITE SUBSCRIBERS, ETC.

WHENEVER YOU MAKE PROGRESS THIS MONTH TOWARDS ONE OF THESE GOALS, COME BACK AND FILL IN A PART OF THE WOLF WITH THE CORRESPONDING COLOR.

DAILY GRATITUDE LOG

WRITE DOWN 3 THINGS YOU ARE GRATEFUL FOR ON EACH LINE

1. ....
2. ....
3. ....
4. ....
5. ....
6. ....
7. ....
8. ....
9. ....
10. ....
11. ....
12. ....
13. ....
14. ....
15. ....
16. ....
17. ....
18. ....
19. ....
20. ....
21. ....
22. ....
23. ....
24. ....
25. ....
26. ....
27. ....
28. ....
29. ....
30. ....
31. ....

WEEKLY GOALS

✗ ....
✗ ....
✗ ....
✗ ....
✗ ....
✗ ....
✗ ....

WEEK SPECIFIC BOUNDARIES

I AM _____
(INSERT AFFIRMATION ABOVE)

This week, I Will Challenge Myself To:

	Mon	Tues	Weds	Thurs	Fri

Weekly Tasks

MON
TUE
WED
THU
FRI

FOR THE
WEEK OF:

RISING RITUAL

I Will Raise My Vibration By:

	Mon	Tues	Wed	Thurs	Fri
_____	○	○	○	○	○
_____	○	○	○	○	○
_____	○	○	○	○	○
_____	○	○	○	○	○
_____	○	○	○	○	○

RITUAL SUGGESTIONS

EARLY RISE/ EARLY SET	GO TECH FREE	PRIORITIZE BALANCE	RECITE MY AFFIRMATIONS	JOURNAL
GO FOR A WALK	MORNING/ EVENING DRINK	SET MILESTONES	BREATHWORK	VISUALIZE SUCCESS
READ	TAKE A HERBAL BATH	EXPRESS GRATITUDE	CLEAN UP	PAMPER MYSELF
UNPLUG	REVIEW GOALS & TO-DO LISTS	WORK DELIBERATELY	SET INTENTIONS	EMBRACE NATURE
FEED MY MIND	EXERCISE	MEDITATE	GET ORGANIZED	LISTEN TO A PODCAST

DON'T OVER STRESS YOURSELF TO AVOID FATIGUE. IT'S NEARLY IMPOSSIBLE TO BE IN A POSITIVE MENTAL STATE WHEN YOUR BODY IS STRESSED OUT.

WEEKLY EXERCISE
THIS WEEK I CHOOSE TO...

- _____
- _____
- _____
- _____
- _____
- _____

WEEKLY FOOD DIARY
LESS OR MORE OF WHAT?

Breakfast:
_____

Lunch:
_____

Dinner:
_____

Snacks:
_____

Beverages:
_____

FITNESS SUGGESTIONS

Do Yoga	Martial Arts	Go for a Walk	Take the Stairs	Eat Less Meat
No sugar	Go Swimming	Dance Party	Team Sports	Yard Work
Do Pilates	Jump Rope	Spin Class	Go Skating	Do Squats
Meat Less Monday	Tae Kwon Do	Do Zumba	Do Tai Chi	Kick Boxing
Ride a Bike	Water Fast	Less Carbs	Go Hiking	Do Cardio

EVENING RITUAL

I Will Maintain My Vibration By: Mon   Tues   Wed   Thurs   Fri

_____

_____

_____

_____

_____

_____

RITUAL SUGGESTIONS LOCATED ON THE RISING RITUALS PAGE

SLEEP CHECK

Getting enough sleep daily ensures you are well rested and ready to tackle the day. Try pushing for seven to eight hours of sleep a night

	SUN	MON	TUE	WED	THU	FRI	SAT
Go to sleep time							
Wake up time							
How long I slept							

WEEKLY REFLECTION

GOALS ACHIEVED:

HIGHLIGHTS:

GOALS FOR NEXT WEEK:

WEEKEND RESTORATION

ADD YOUR WEEKEND SELF CARE PLANS BELOW

-
-
-

WEEKLY GOALS

- ✗ ....
- ✗ ....
- ✗ ....
- ✗ ....
- ✗ ....
- ✗ ....
- ✗ ....

WEEK SPECIFIC BOUNDARIES

I AM _____
(INSERT AFFIRMATION ABOVE)

This week, I Will Challenge Myself To:	Mon	Tues	Weds	Thurs	Fri

Weekly Tasks

MON
TUE
WED
THU
FRI

FOR THE
WEEK OF:

RISING RITUAL

I Will Raise My Vibration By:

	Mon	Tues	Wed	Thurs	Fri
_____	○	○	○	○	○
_____	○	○	○	○	○
_____	○	○	○	○	○
_____	○	○	○	○	○
_____	○	○	○	○	○

RITUAL SUGGESTIONS

EARLY RISE/ EARLY SET	GO TECH FREE	PRIORITIZE BALANCE	RECITE YOUR AFFIRMATIONS	JOURNAL
GO FOR A WALK	MORNING/ EVENING DRINK	SET MILESTONES	BREATHWORK	VISUALIZE SUCCESS
READ	TAKE A HERBAL BATH	EXPRESS GRATITUDE	CLEAN UP	PAMPER YOURSELF
UNPLUG	REVIEW GOALS & TO-DO LISTS	WORK DELIBERATELY	SET INTENTIONS	EMBRACE NATURE
FEED YOUR MIND	EXERCISE	MEDITATE	GET ORGANIZED	LISTEN TO A PODCAST

DON'T OVER STRESS YOURSELF TO AVOID FATIGUE. IT'S NEARLY IMPOSSIBLE TO BE IN A POSITIVE MENTAL STATE WHEN YOUR BODY IS STRESSED OUT.

WEEKLY EXERCISE
THIS WEEK I CHOOSE TO...

- _____
- _____
- _____
- _____
- _____
- _____

WEEKLY FOOD DIARY
LESS OR MORE OF WHAT?

Breakfast:
_____

Lunch:
_____

Dinner:
_____

Snacks:
_____

Beverages:
_____

FITNESS SUGGESTIONS

Do Yoga	Martial Arts	Go for a Walk	Take the Stairs	Eat Less Meat
No sugar	Go Swimming	Dance Party	Team Sports	Yard Work
Do Pilates	Jump Rope	Spin Class	Go Skating	Do Squats
Meat Less Monday	Tae Kwon Do	Do Zumba	Do Tai Chi	Kick Boxing
Ride a Bike	Water Fast	Less Carbs	Go Hiking	Do Cardio

EVENING RITUAL

I Will Maintain My Vibration By:

	Mon	Tues	Wed	Thurs	Fri
_____	○	○	○	○	○
_____	○	○	○	○	○
_____	○	○	○	○	○
_____	○	○	○	○	○
_____	○	○	○	○	○
_____	○	○	○	○	○

RITUAL SUGGESTIONS LOCATED ON THE RISING RITUALS PAGE

SLEEP CHECK

Getting enough sleep daily ensures you are well rested and ready to tackle the day. Try pushing for seven to eight hours of sleep a night

	SUN	MON	TUE	WED	THU	FRI	SAT
Go to sleep time							
Wake up time							
How long I slept							

WEEKLY REFLECTION

_____
_____
_____
_____

GOALS ACHIEVED:

HIGHLIGHTS:

GOALS FOR NEXT WEEK:

WEEKEND RESTORATION
ADD YOUR WEEKEND SELF CARE PLANS BELOW

-
-
-

WEEKLY GOALS

- ✗ ....
- ✗ ....
- ✗ ....
- ✗ ....
- ✗ ....
- ✗ ....
- ✗ ....

WEEK SPECIFIC BOUNDARIES | I AM _____
(INSERT AFFIRMATION ABOVE)

This week, I Will Challenge Myself To:

	Mon	Tues	Weds	Thurs	Fri

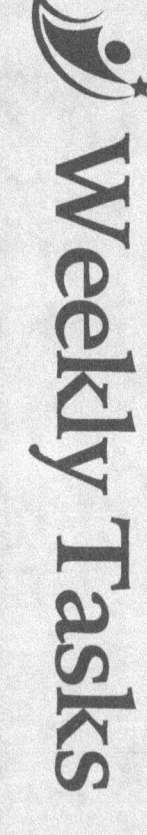

Weekly Tasks

MON
TUE
WED
THU
FRI

FOR THE
WEEK OF:

RISING RITUAL

I Will Raise My Vibration By:

	Mon	Tues	Wed	Thurs	Fri
_____	○	○	○	○	○
_____	○	○	○	○	○
_____	○	○	○	○	○
_____	○	○	○	○	○
_____	○	○	○	○	○

RITUAL SUGGESTIONS

EARLY RISE/ EARLY SET	GO TECH FREE	PRIORITIZE BALANCE	RECITE YOUR AFFIRMATIONS	JOURNAL
GO FOR A WALK	MORNING/ EVENING DRINK	SET MILESTONES	BREATHWORK	VISUALIZE SUCCESS
READ	TAKE A HERBAL BATH	EXPRESS GRATITUDE	CLEAN UP	PAMPER YOURSELF
UNPLUG	REVIEW GOALS & TO-DO LISTS	WORK DELIBERATELY	SET INTENTIONS	EMBRACE NATURE
FEED YOUR MIND	EXERCISE	MEDITATE	GET ORGANIZED	LISTEN TO A PODCAST

DON'T OVER STRESS YOURSELF TO AVOID FATIGUE. IT'S NEARLY IMPOSSIBLE TO BE IN A POSITIVE MENTAL STATE WHEN YOUR BODY IS STRESSED OUT.

WEEKLY EXERCISE
THIS WEEK I CHOOSE TO...

- _____
- _____
- _____
- _____
- _____
- _____

WEEKLY FOOD DIARY
LESS OR MORE OF WHAT?

Breakfast:

Lunch:

Dinner:

Snacks:

Beverages:

FITNESS SUGGESTIONS

Do Yoga	Martial Arts	Go for a Walk	Take the Stairs	Eat Less Meat
No sugar	Go Swimming	Dance Party	Team Sports	Yard Work
Do Pilates	Jump Rope	Spin Class	Go Skating	Do Squats
Meat Less Monday	Tae Kwon Do	Do Zumba	Do Tai Chi	Kick Boxing
Ride a Bike	Water Fast	Less Carbs	Go Hiking	Do Cardio

EVENING RITUAL

I Will Maintain My Vibration By:	Mon	Tues	Wed	Thurs	Fri
_____	○	○	○	○	○
_____	○	○	○	○	○
_____	○	○	○	○	○
_____	○	○	○	○	○
_____	○	○	○	○	○
_____	○	○	○	○	○

RITUAL SUGGESTIONS LOCATED ON THE RISING RITUALS PAGE

SLEEP CHECK

Getting enough sleep daily ensures you are well rested and ready to tackle the day. Try pushing for seven to eight hours of sleep a night

	SUN	MON	TUE	WED	THU	FRI	SAT
Go to sleep time							
Wake up time							
How long I slept							

WEEKLY REFLECTION

GOALS ACHIEVED:

HIGHLIGHTS:

GOALS FOR NEXT WEEK:

WEEKEND RESTORATION

ADD YOUR WEEKEND SELF CARE PLANS BELOW

WEEKLY GOALS

- ✗ ....
- ✗ ....
- ✗ ....
- ✗ ....
- ✗ ....
- ✗ ....
- ✗ ....

WEEK SPECIFIC BOUNDARIES | I AM _____
(INSERT AFFIRMATION ABOVE)

This week, I Will Challenge Myself To:

	Mon	Tues	Weds	Thurs	Fri

Weekly Tasks

MON TUE WED THU FRI

FOR THE
WEEK OF:

RISING RITUAL

I Will Raise My Vibration By: | Mon | Tues | Wed | Thurs | Fri

_____

_____

_____

_____

_____

EARLY RISE/ EARLY SET	GO TECH FREE	PRIORITIZE BALANCE	RECITE YOUR AFFIRMATIONS	JOURNAL
GO FOR A WALK	MORNING/ EVENING DRINK	SET MILESTONES	BREATHWORK	VISUALIZE SUCCESS
READ	TAKE A HERBAL BATH	EXPRESS GRATITUDE	CLEAN UP	PAMPER YOURSELF
UNPLUG	REVIEW GOALS & TO-DO LISTS	WORK DELIBERATELY	SET INTENTIONS	EMBRACE NATURE
FEED YOUR MIND	EXERCISE	MEDITATE	GET ORGANIZED	LISTEN TO A PODCAST

RITUAL SUGGESTIONS

DON'T OVER STRESS YOURSELF TO AVOID FATIGUE. IT'S NEARLY IMPOSSIBLE TO BE IN A POSITIVE MENTAL STATE WHEN YOUR BODY IS STRESSED OUT.

WEEKLY EXERCISE
THIS WEEK I CHOOSE TO...

- _____
- _____
- _____
- _____
- _____
- _____

WEEKLY FOOD DIARY
LESS OR MORE OF WHAT?

Breakfast:
_____

Lunch:
_____

Dinner:
_____

Snacks:
_____

Beverages:
_____

FITNESS SUGGESTIONS

Do Yoga	Martial Arts	Go for a Walk	Take the Stairs	Eat Less Meat
No sugar	Go Swimming	Dance Party	Team Sports	Yard Work
Do Pilates	Jump Rope	Spin Class	Go Skating	Do Squats
Meat Less Monday	Tae Kwon Do	Do Zumba	Do Tai Chi	Kick Boxing
Ride a Bike	Water Fast	Less Carbs	Go Hiking	Do Cardio

EVENING RITUAL

I Will Maintain My Vibration By: Mon   Tues   Wed   Thurs   Fri

_____

_____

_____

_____

_____

_____

RITUAL SUGGESTIONS LOCATED ON THE RISING RITUALS PAGE

SLEEP CHECK

Getting enough sleep daily ensures you are well rested and ready to tackle the day. Try pushing for seven to eight hours of sleep a night

	SUN	MON	TUE	WED	THU	FRI	SAT
Go to sleep time							
Wake up time							
How long I slept							

WEEKLY REFLECTION

_____
_____
_____

GOALS ACHIEVED:

HIGHLIGHTS:

GOALS FOR NEXT WEEK:

WEEKEND RESTORATION

ADD YOUR WEEKEND SELF CARE PLANS BELOW

END OF MONTH RECAP

SMALL WINS
1. _____
2. _____
3. _____

BIG ACHIEVEMENTS
1. _____
2. _____
3. _____

HIGHLIGHTS

LESSONS I LEARNED

WHAT WORKED

WHAT I'LL STOP DOING

IMPROVEMENTS TO MAKE

M	T	W	T	F	S	S

Top Priorities

_____
_____
_____
_____
_____
_____
_____
_____
_____

Notes

MONTHLY GOALS

MY FOCUS IS ON

MILESTONES
1
2
3

DO   DON'T

MAIN GOALS
1
2
3
4
5

IMPORTANT DATES

GOAL SUGGESTIONS

REACH OUT TO AN INFLUENCER	HEALTHY WORK/LIFE BALANCE	PRACTICE CONFIDENCE	EMAIL 10 NEW PROSPECTS ABOUT MY BUSINESS	LET GO OF LIMITING BELIEFS	IMPROVE CUSTOMER ENGAGEMENT
WORK ON MY SOCIAL MEDIA PRESENCE	PRACTICE DECISVENESS	LEARN A NEW SKILL	INCREASE SALES	PRACTICE MINDFULNESS	REDUCE BUSINESS EXPENSES
FIND NEW HOBBIES	WORK ON MY MARKETING STRATEGY	DELEGATE EFFECTIVELY	STAND UP TO MY FEARS	WORK WITH IDEAL CLIENTS	PLAN MY MARKETING CALENDAR

MONTHLY BUDGET

MONTH OF: _____

\multicolumn{4}{c|}{INCOME}			
DATE	SOURCE	CATEGORY	AMOUNT

BILLS & FIXED EXPENSES		
DATE	SOURCE	AMOUNT

VARIABLE EXPENSES		
DATE	SOURCE	AMOUNT

SUMMARY	
SOURCE	AMOUNT
INCOME	
BILLS & FIXED EXPENSES	
VARIABLE EXPENSES	
BALANCE	

SOCIAL MEDIA POSTING SCHEDULE

Test out the three social media networks you chose to focus on

Month: _____   **Monthly Focus:** _____

NETWORK	SUN	MON	TUE	WED	THU	FRI	SAT

NETWORK	SUN	MON	TUE	WED	THU	FRI	SAT

NETWORK	SUN	MON	TUE	WED	THU	FRI	SAT

NETWORK	SUN	MON	TUE	WED	THU	FRI	SAT

PROGRESS TRACKER

KEY

START BY COLORING IN EACH BOX IN THE GRAY KEY AREA WITH A DIFFERENT COLOR. NEXT TO THE BOX, YOU WILL CREATE PERFORMANCE METRICS FOR THE MONTH.
FOR EX: PROJECTS COMPLETED, NEW CLIENTS, RETURNING CLIENTS, SOCIAL MEDIA GROWTH, SALES, WEBSITE SUBSCRIBERS, ETC.

WHENEVER YOU MAKE PROGRESS THIS MONTH TOWARDS ONE OF THESE GOALS, COME BACK AND FILL IN A PART OF THE WOLF WITH THE CORRESPONDING COLOR.

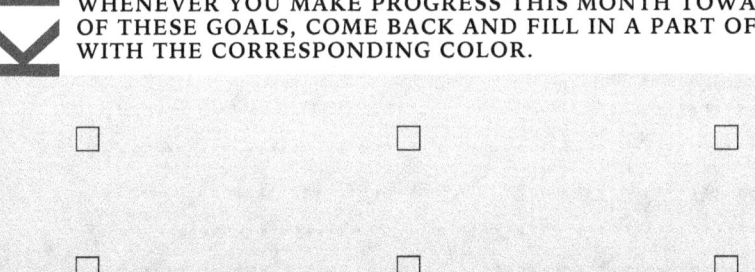

DAILY GRATITUDE LOG

WRITE DOWN 3 THINGS YOU ARE GRATEFUL FOR ON EACH LINE

1. ....
2. ....
3. ....
4. ....
5. ....
6. ....
7. ....
8. ....
9. ....
10. ....
11. ....
12. ....
13. ....
14. ....
15. ....
16. ....
17. ....
18. ....
19. ....
20. ....
21. ....
22. ....
23. ....
24. ....
25. ....
26. ....
27. ....
28. ....
29. ....
30. ....
31. ....

WEEKLY GOALS

- ✗ ....
- ✗ ....
- ✗ ....
- ✗ ....
- ✗ ....
- ✗ ....
- ✗ ....

WEEK SPECIFIC BOUNDARIES

I AM _____
(INSERT AFFIRMATION ABOVE)

This week, I Will Challenge Myself To:	Mon	Tues	Weds	Thurs	Fri

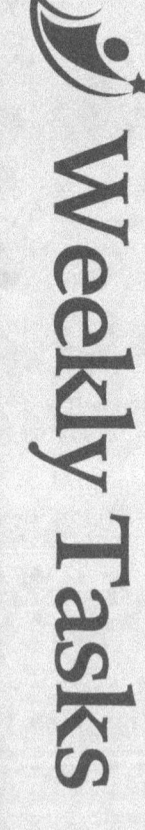

Weekly Tasks

MON
TUE
WED
THU
FRI

FOR THE
WEEK OF:

RISING RITUAL

I Will Raise My Vibration By: Mon   Tues   Wed   Thurs   Fri

_____

_____

_____

_____

_____

RITUAL SUGGESTIONS

EARLY RISE/ EARLY SET	GO TECH FREE	PRIORITIZE BALANCE	RECITE MY AFFIRMATIONS	JOURNAL
GO FOR A WALK	MORNING/ EVENING DRINK	SET MILESTONES	BREATHWORK	VISUALIZE SUCCESS
READ	TAKE A HERBAL BATH	EXPRESS GRATITUDE	CLEAN UP	PAMPER MYSELF
UNPLUG	REVIEW GOALS & TO-DO LISTS	WORK DELIBERATELY	SET INTENTIONS	EMBRACE NATURE
FEED MY MIND	EXERCISE	MEDITATE	GET ORGANIZED	LISTEN TO A PODCAST

DON'T OVER STRESS YOURSELF TO AVOID FATIGUE. IT'S NEARLY IMPOSSIBLE TO BE IN A POSITIVE MENTAL STATE WHEN YOUR BODY IS STRESSED OUT.

WEEKLY EXERCISE
THIS WEEK I CHOOSE TO...

- _____
- _____
- _____
- _____
- _____
- _____
- _____

WEEKLY FOOD DIARY
LESS OR MORE OF WHAT?

Breakfast:

Lunch:

Dinner:

Snacks:

Beverages:

FITNESS SUGGESTIONS

Do Yoga	Martial Arts	Go for a Walk	Take the Stairs	Eat Less Meat
No sugar	Go Swimming	Dance Party	Team Sports	Yard Work
Do Pilates	Jump Rope	Spin Class	Go Skating	Do Squats
Meat Less Monday	Tae Kwon Do	Do Zumba	Do Tai Chi	Kick Boxing
Ride a Bike	Water Fast	Less Carbs	Go Hiking	Do Cardio

EVENING RITUAL

I Will Maintain My Vibration By:	Mon	Tues	Wed	Thurs	Fri
_____	○	○	○	○	○
_____	○	○	○	○	○
_____	○	○	○	○	○
_____	○	○	○	○	○
_____	○	○	○	○	○
_____	○	○	○	○	○

RITUAL SUGGESTIONS LOCATED ON THE RISING RITUALS PAGE

SLEEP CHECK

Getting enough sleep daily ensures you are well rested and ready to tackle the day. Try pushing for seven to eight hours of sleep a night

	SUN	MON	TUE	WED	THU	FRI	SAT
Go to sleep time							
Wake up time							
How long I slept							

WEEKLY REFLECTION

GOALS ACHIEVED:

HIGHLIGHTS:

GOALS FOR NEXT WEEK:

WEEKEND RESTORATION

ADD YOUR WEEKEND SELF CARE PLANS BELOW

WEEKLY GOALS

- ✗ ....
- ✗ ....
- ✗ ....
- ✗ ....
- ✗ ....
- ✗ ....
- ✗ ....

WEEK SPECIFIC BOUNDARIES

I AM _____
(INSERT AFFIRMATION ABOVE)

This week, I Will Challenge Myself To:	Mon	Tues	Weds	Thurs	Fri

Weekly Tasks

	MON	TUE	WED	THU	FRI

FOR THE WEEK OF:

RISING RITUAL

I Will Raise My Vibration By:

	Mon	Tues	Wed	Thurs	Fri
_____	○	○	○	○	○
_____	○	○	○	○	○
_____	○	○	○	○	○
_____	○	○	○	○	○
_____	○	○	○	○	○
_____	○	○	○	○	○

RITUAL SUGGESTIONS

EARLY RISE/ EARLY SET	GO TECH FREE	PRIORITIZE BALANCE	RECITE YOUR AFFIRMATIONS	JOURNAL
GO FOR A WALK	MORNING/ EVENING DRINK	SET MILESTONES	BREATHWORK	VISUALIZE SUCCESS
READ	TAKE A HERBAL BATH	EXPRESS GRATITUDE	CLEAN UP	PAMPER YOURSELF
UNPLUG	REVIEW GOALS & TO-DO LISTS	WORK DELIBERATELY	SET INTENTIONS	EMBRACE NATURE
FEED YOUR MIND	EXERCISE	MEDITATE	GET ORGANIZED	LISTEN TO A PODCAST

DON'T OVER STRESS YOURSELF TO AVOID FATIGUE. IT'S NEARLY IMPOSSIBLE TO BE IN A POSITIVE MENTAL STATE WHEN YOUR BODY IS STRESSED OUT.

WEEKLY EXERCISE
THIS WEEK I CHOOSE TO...

- _____
- _____
- _____
- _____
- _____
- _____

WEEKLY FOOD DIARY
LESS OR MORE OF WHAT?

Breakfast:

Lunch:

Dinner:

Snacks:

Beverages:

FITNESS SUGGESTIONS

Do Yoga	Martial Arts	Go for a Walk	Take the Stairs	Eat Less Meat
No sugar	Go Swimming	Dance Party	Team Sports	Yard Work
Do Pilates	Jump Rope	Spin Class	Go Skating	Do Squats
Meat Less Monday	Tae Kwon Do	Do Zumba	Do Tai Chi	Kick Boxing
Ride a Bike	Water Fast	Less Carbs	Go Hiking	Do Cardio

EVENING RITUAL

I Will Maintain My Vibration By: Mon   Tues   Wed   Thurs   Fri

_____

_____

_____

_____

_____

_____

RITUAL SUGGESTIONS LOCATED ON THE RISING RITUALS PAGE

SLEEP CHECK

Getting enough sleep daily ensures you are well rested and ready to tackle the day. Try pushing for seven to eight hours of sleep a night

	SUN	MON	TUE	WED	THU	FRI	SAT
Go to sleep time							
Wake up time							
How long I slept							

WEEKLY REFLECTION

_____
_____
_____

GOALS ACHIEVED:

HIGHLIGHTS:

GOALS FOR NEXT WEEK:

WEEKEND RESTORATION
ADD YOUR WEEKEND SELF CARE PLANS BELOW

WEEKLY GOALS

- ✗ ....
- ✗ ....
- ✗ ....
- ✗ ....
- ✗ ....
- ✗ ....
- ✗ ....

WEEK SPECIFIC BOUNDARIES

I AM _____
(INSERT AFFIRMATION ABOVE)

This week, I Will Challenge Myself To:	Mon	Tues	Weds	Thurs	Fri

Weekly Tasks

	MON	TUE	WED	THU	FRI

FOR THE
WEEK OF:

RISING RITUAL

I Will Raise My Vibration By: **Mon**   **Tues**   **Wed**   **Thurs**   **Fri**

_____

_____

_____

_____

_____

RITUAL SUGGESTIONS

EARLY RISE/ EARLY SET	GO TECH FREE	PRIORITIZE BALANCE	RECITE YOUR AFFIRMATIONS	JOURNAL
GO FOR A WALK	MORNING/ EVENING DRINK	SET MILESTONES	BREATHWORK	VISUALIZE SUCCESS
READ	TAKE A HERBAL BATH	EXPRESS GRATITUDE	CLEAN UP	PAMPER YOURSELF
UNPLUG	REVIEW GOALS & TO-DO LISTS	WORK DELIBERATELY	SET INTENTIONS	EMBRACE NATURE
FEED YOUR MIND	EXERCISE	MEDITATE	GET ORGANIZED	LISTEN TO A PODCAST

DON'T OVER STRESS YOURSELF TO AVOID FATIGUE. IT'S NEARLY IMPOSSIBLE TO BE IN A POSITIVE MENTAL STATE WHEN YOUR BODY IS STRESSED OUT.

WEEKLY EXERCISE
THIS WEEK I CHOOSE TO...

- _____
- _____
- _____
- _____
- _____
- _____

WEEKLY FOOD DIARY
LESS OR MORE OF WHAT?

Breakfast:

Lunch:

Dinner:

Snacks:

Beverages:

FITNESS SUGGESTIONS

Do Yoga	Martial Arts	Go for a Walk	Take the Stairs	Eat Less Meat
No sugar	Go Swimming	Dance Party	Team Sports	Yard Work
Do Pilates	Jump Rope	Spin Class	Go Skating	Do Squats
Meat Less Monday	Tae Kwon Do	Do Zumba	Do Tai Chi	Kick Boxing
Ride a Bike	Water Fast	Less Carbs	Go Hiking	Do Cardio

EVENING RITUAL

I Will Maintain My Vibration By: Mon   Tues   Wed   Thurs   Fri

_____

_____

_____

_____

_____

_____

RITUAL SUGGESTIONS LOCATED ON THE RISING RITUALS PAGE

SLEEP CHECK

Getting enough sleep daily ensures you are well rested and ready to tackle the day. Try pushing for seven to eight hours of sleep a night

	SUN	MON	TUE	WED	THU	FRI	SAT
Go to sleep time							
Wake up time							
How long I slept							

WEEKLY REFLECTION

_____
_____
_____

GOALS ACHIEVED:

HIGHLIGHTS:

GOALS FOR NEXT WEEK:

WEEKEND RESTORATION

ADD YOUR WEEKEND SELF CARE PLANS BELOW

-
-
-

WEEKLY GOALS

- ✗ ....
- ✗ ....
- ✗ ....
- ✗ ....
- ✗ ....
- ✗ ....
- ✗ ....

WEEK SPECIFIC BOUNDARIES

I AM _____
(INSERT AFFIRMATION ABOVE)

This week, I Will Challenge Myself To:

	Mon	Tues	Weds	Thurs	Fri

Weekly Tasks

MON

TUE

WED

THU

FRI

FOR THE
WEEK OF:

RISING RITUAL

I Will Raise My Vibration By: **Mon**   **Tues**   **Wed**   **Thurs**   **Fri**

_____

_____

_____

_____

_____

RITUAL SUGGESTIONS

EARLY RISE/ EARLY SET	GO TECH FREE	PRIORITIZE BALANCE	RECITE YOUR AFFIRMATIONS	JOURNAL
GO FOR A WALK	MORNING/ EVENING DRINK	SET MILESTONES	BREATHWORK	VISUALIZE SUCCESS
READ	TAKE A HERBAL BATH	EXPRESS GRATITUDE	CLEAN UP	PAMPER YOURSELF
UNPLUG	REVIEW GOALS & TO-DO LISTS	WORK DELIBERATELY	SET INTENTIONS	EMBRACE NATURE
FEED YOUR MIND	EXERCISE	MEDITATE	GET ORGANIZED	LISTEN TO A PODCAST

DON'T OVER STRESS YOURSELF TO AVOID FATIGUE. IT'S NEARLY IMPOSSIBLE TO BE IN A POSITIVE MENTAL STATE WHEN YOUR BODY IS STRESSED OUT.

WEEKLY EXERCISE
THIS WEEK I CHOOSE TO...

- _____
- _____
- _____
- _____
- _____
- _____

WEEKLY FOOD DIARY
LESS OR MORE OF WHAT?

Breakfast: _____

Lunch: _____

Dinner: _____

Snacks: _____

Beverages: _____

FITNESS SUGGESTIONS

Do Yoga	Martial Arts	Go for a Walk	Take the Stairs	Eat Less Meat
No sugar	Go Swimming	Dance Party	Team Sports	Yard Work
Do Pilates	Jump Rope	Spin Class	Go Skating	Do Squats
Meat Less Monday	Tae Kwon Do	Do Zumba	Do Tai Chi	Kick Boxing
Ride a Bike	Water Fast	Less Carbs	Go Hiking	Do Cardio

EVENING RITUAL

I Will Maintain My Vibration By: | Mon | Tues | Wed | Thurs | Fri

_____

_____

_____

_____

_____

_____

RITUAL SUGGESTIONS LOCATED ON THE RISING RITUALS PAGE

SLEEP CHECK

Getting enough sleep daily ensures you are well rested and ready to tackle the day. Try pushing for seven to eight hours of sleep a night

	SUN	MON	TUE	WED	THU	FRI	SAT
Go to sleep time							
Wake up time							
How long I slept							

WEEKLY REFLECTION

GOALS ACHIEVED:

HIGHLIGHTS:

GOALS FOR NEXT WEEK:

WEEKEND RESTORATION

ADD YOUR WEEKEND SELF CARE PLANS BELOW

-
-
-

END OF MONTH RECAP

SMALL WINS
1. _____
2. _____
3. _____

BIG ACHIEVEMENTS
1. _____
2. _____
3. _____

HIGHLIGHTS

LESSONS I LEARNED

WHAT WORKED

WHAT I'LL STOP DOING

IMPROVEMENTS TO MAKE

M	T	W	T	F	S	S

Top Priorities

_____
_____
_____
_____
_____
_____
_____
_____
_____

Notes

MONTHLY GOALS

MY FOCUS IS ON

MILESTONES
1.
2.
3.

DO   DON'T

MAIN GOALS
1.
2.
3.
4.
5.

IMPORTANT DATES

GOAL SUGGESTIONS

REACH OUT TO AN INFLUENCER	HEALTHY WORK/LIFE BALANCE	PRACTICE CONFIDENCE	EMAIL 10 NEW PROSPECTS ABOUT MY BUSINESS	LET GO OF LIMITING BELIEFS	IMPROVE CUSTOMER ENGAGEMENT
WORK ON MY SOCIAL MEDIA PRESENCE	PRACTICE DECISVENESS	LEARN A NEW SKILL	INCREASE SALES	PRACTICE MINDFULNESS	REDUCE BUSINESS EXPENSES
FIND NEW HOBBIES	WORK ON MY MARKETING STRATEGY	DELEGATE EFFECTIVELY	STAND UP TO MY FEARS	WORK WITH IDEAL CLIENTS	PLAN MY MARKETING CALENDAR

MONTHLY BUDGET

MONTH OF: _____

INCOME			
DATE	SOURCE	CATEGORY	AMOUNT

BILLS & FIXED EXPENSES		
DATE	SOURCE	AMOUNT

VARIABLE EXPENSES		
DATE	SOURCE	AMOUNT

SUMMARY	
SOURCE	AMOUNT
INCOME	
BILLS & FIXED EXPENSES	
VARIABLE EXPENSES	
BALANCE	

SOCIAL MEDIA POSTING SCHEDULE

Test out the three social media networks you chose to focus on

Month: _____ **Monthly Focus:** _____

NETWORK	SUN	MON	TUE	WED	THU	FRI	SAT

NETWORK	SUN	MON	TUE	WED	THU	FRI	SAT

NETWORK	SUN	MON	TUE	WED	THU	FRI	SAT

NETWORK	SUN	MON	TUE	WED	THU	FRI	SAT

PROGRESS TRACKER

START BY COLORING IN EACH BOX IN THE GRAY KEY AREA WITH A DIFFERENT COLOR. NEXT TO THE BOX, YOU WILL CREATE PERFORMANCE METRICS FOR THE MONTH.
FOR EX: PROJECTS COMPLETED, NEW CLIENTS, RETURNING CLIENTS, SOCIAL MEDIA GROWTH, SALES, WEBSITE SUBSCRIBERS, ETC.

WHENEVER YOU MAKE PROGRESS THIS MONTH TOWARDS ONE OF THESE GOALS, COME BACK AND FILL IN A PART OF THE WOLF WITH THE CORRESPONDING COLOR.

KEY

DAILY GRATITUDE LOG

WRITE DOWN 3 THINGS YOU ARE GRATEFUL FOR ON EACH LINE

1. ....
2. ....
3. ....
4. ....
5. ....
6. ....
7. ....
8. ....
9. ....
10. ....
11. ....
12. ....
13. ....
14. ....
15. ....
16. ....
17. ....
18. ....
19. ....
20. ....
21. ....
22. ....
23. ....
24. ....
25. ....
26. ....
27. ....
28. ....
29. ....
30. ....
31. ....

WEEKLY GOALS

- ✗ ....
- ✗ ....
- ✗ ....
- ✗ ....
- ✗ ....
- ✗ ....
- ✗ ....

WEEK SPECIFIC BOUNDARIES

I AM _____
(INSERT AFFIRMATION ABOVE)

This week, I Will Challenge Myself To:

	Mon	Tues	Wcds	Thurs	Fri

Weekly Tasks

MON TUE WED THU FRI

FOR THE
WEEK OF:

RISING RITUAL

I Will Raise My Vibration By:

	Mon	Tues	Wed	Thurs	Fri
_____	○	○	○	○	○
_____	○	○	○	○	○
_____	○	○	○	○	○
_____	○	○	○	○	○
_____	○	○	○	○	○

RITUAL SUGGESTIONS

EARLY RISE/ EARLY SET	GO TECH FREE	PRIORITIZE BALANCE	RECITE MY AFFIRMATIONS	JOURNAL
GO FOR A WALK	MORNING/ EVENING DRINK	SET MILESTONES	BREATHWORK	VISUALIZE SUCCESS
READ	TAKE A HERBAL BATH	EXPRESS GRATITUDE	CLEAN UP	PAMPER MYSELF
UNPLUG	REVIEW GOALS & TO-DO LISTS	WORK DELIBERATELY	SET INTENTIONS	EMBRACE NATURE
FEED MY MIND	EXERCISE	MEDITATE	GET ORGANIZED	LISTEN TO A PODCAST

DON'T OVER STRESS YOURSELF TO AVOID FATIGUE. IT'S NEARLY IMPOSSIBLE TO BE IN A POSITIVE MENTAL STATE WHEN YOUR BODY IS STRESSED OUT.

WEEKLY EXERCISE
THIS WEEK I CHOOSE TO...

- _____
- _____
- _____
- _____
- _____
- _____

WEEKLY FOOD DIARY
LESS OR MORE OF WHAT?

Breakfast:

Lunch:

Dinner:

Snacks:

Beverages:

FITNESS SUGGESTIONS

Do Yoga	Martial Arts	Go for a Walk	Take the Stairs	Eat Less Meat
No sugar	Go Swimming	Dance Party	Team Sports	Yard Work
Do Pilates	Jump Rope	Spin Class	Go Skating	Do Squats
Meat Less Monday	Tae Kwon Do	Do Zumba	Do Tai Chi	Kick Boxing
Ride a Bike	Water Fast	Less Carbs	Go Hiking	Do Cardio

EVENING RITUAL

I Will Maintain My Vibration By:	Mon	Tues	Wed	Thurs	Fri
_____	○	○	○	○	○
_____	○	○	○	○	○
_____	○	○	○	○	○
_____	○	○	○	○	○
_____	○	○	○	○	○
_____	○	○	○	○	○

RITUAL SUGGESTIONS LOCATED ON THE RISING RITUALS PAGE

SLEEP CHECK

Getting enough sleep daily ensures you are well rested and ready to tackle the day. Try pushing for seven to eight hours of sleep a night

	SUN	MON	TUE	WED	THU	FRI	SAT
Go to sleep time							
Wake up time							
How long I slept							

WEEKLY REFLECTION

GOALS ACHIEVED:

HIGHLIGHTS:

GOALS FOR NEXT WEEK:

WEEKEND RESTORATION
ADD YOUR WEEKEND SELF CARE PLANS BELOW

WEEKLY GOALS

- ✘ ....
- ✘ ....
- ✘ ....
- ✘ ....
- ✘ ....
- ✘ ....
- ✘ ....

WEEK SPECIFIC BOUNDARIES | I AM _____
(INSERT AFFIRMATION ABOVE)

This week, I Will Challenge Myself To:

	Mon	Tues	Weds	Thurs	Fri

Weekly Tasks

MON TUE WED THU FRI

FOR THE
WEEK OF:

RISING RITUAL

I Will Raise My Vibration By:

	Mon	Tues	Wed	Thurs	Fri
_____	○	○	○	○	○
_____	○	○	○	○	○
_____	○	○	○	○	○
_____	○	○	○	○	○
_____	○	○	○	○	○

RITUAL SUGGESTIONS

EARLY RISE/ EARLY SET	GO TECH FREE	PRIORITIZE BALANCE	RECITE YOUR AFFIRMATIONS	JOURNAL
GO FOR A WALK	MORNING/ EVENING DRINK	SET MILESTONES	BREATHWORK	VISUALIZE SUCCESS
READ	TAKE A HERBAL BATH	EXPRESS GRATITUDE	CLEAN UP	PAMPER YOURSELF
UNPLUG	REVIEW GOALS & TO-DO LISTS	WORK DELIBERATELY	SET INTENTIONS	EMBRACE NATURE
FEED YOUR MIND	EXERCISE	MEDITATE	GET ORGANIZED	LISTEN TO A PODCAST

DON'T OVER STRESS YOURSELF TO AVOID FATIGUE. IT'S NEARLY IMPOSSIBLE TO BE IN A POSITIVE MENTAL STATE WHEN YOUR BODY IS STRESSED OUT.

WEEKLY EXERCISE
THIS WEEK I CHOOSE TO...

- _____
- _____
- _____
- _____
- _____
- _____

WEEKLY FOOD DIARY
LESS OR MORE OF WHAT?

Breakfast:
_____

Lunch:
_____

Dinner:
_____

Snacks:
_____

Beverages:
_____

FITNESS SUGGESTIONS

Do Yoga	Martial Arts	Go for a Walk	Take the Stairs	Eat Less Meat
No sugar	Go Swimming	Dance Party	Team Sports	Yard Work
Do Pilates	Jump Rope	Spin Class	Go Skating	Do Squats
Meat Less Monday	Tae Kwon Do	Do Zumba	Do Tai Chi	Kick Boxing
Ride a Bike	Water Fast	Less Carbs	Go Hiking	Do Cardio

EVENING RITUAL

I Will Maintain My Vibration By:	Mon	Tues	Wed	Thurs	Fri
_____	○	○	○	○	○
_____	○	○	○	○	○
_____	○	○	○	○	○
_____	○	○	○	○	○
_____	○	○	○	○	○
_____	○	○	○	○	○

RITUAL SUGGESTIONS LOCATED ON THE RISING RITUALS PAGE

SLEEP CHECK

Getting enough sleep daily ensures you are well rested and ready to tackle the day. Try pushing for seven to eight hours of sleep a night

	SUN	MON	TUE	WED	THU	FRI	SAT
Go to sleep time							
Wake up time							
How long I slept							

WEEKLY REFLECTION

GOALS ACHIEVED:

HIGHLIGHTS:

GOALS FOR NEXT WEEK:

WEEKEND RESTORATION
ADD YOUR WEEKEND SELF CARE PLANS BELOW

WEEKLY GOALS

- ✗ ....
- ✗ ....
- ✗ ....
- ✗ ....
- ✗ ....
- ✗ ....
- ✗ ....

WEEK SPECIFIC BOUNDARIES | I AM _____
(INSERT AFFIRMATION ABOVE)

This week, I Will Challenge Myself To:	Mon	Tues	Weds	Thurs	Fri

Weekly Tasks

	MON	TUE	WED	THU	FRI

FOR THE WEEK OF:

RISING RITUAL

I Will Raise My Vibration By:

	Mon	Tues	Wed	Thurs	Fri
_____	○	○	○	○	○
_____	○	○	○	○	○
_____	○	○	○	○	○
_____	○	○	○	○	○
_____	○	○	○	○	○

RITUAL SUGGESTIONS

EARLY RISE/ EARLY SET	GO TECH FREE	PRIORITIZE BALANCE	RECITE YOUR AFFIRMATIONS	JOURNAL
GO FOR A WALK	MORNING/ EVENING DRINK	SET MILESTONES	BREATHWORK	VISUALIZE SUCCESS
READ	TAKE A HERBAL BATH	EXPRESS GRATITUDE	CLEAN UP	PAMPER YOURSELF
UNPLUG	REVIEW GOALS & TO-DO LISTS	WORK DELIBERATELY	SET INTENTIONS	EMBRACE NATURE
FEED YOUR MIND	EXERCISE	MEDITATE	GET ORGANIZED	LISTEN TO A PODCAST

DON'T OVER STRESS YOURSELF TO AVOID FATIGUE. IT'S NEARLY IMPOSSIBLE TO BE IN A POSITIVE MENTAL STATE WHEN YOUR BODY IS STRESSED OUT.

WEEKLY EXERCISE
THIS WEEK I CHOOSE TO...

- _____
- _____
- _____
- _____
- _____
- _____

WEEKLY FOOD DIARY
LESS OR MORE OF WHAT?

Breakfast:
_____

Lunch:
_____

Dinner:
_____

Snacks:
_____

Beverages:
_____

FITNESS SUGGESTIONS

Do Yoga	Martial Arts	Go for a Walk	Take the Stairs	Eat Less Meat
No sugar	Go Swimming	Dance Party	Team Sports	Yard Work
Do Pilates	Jump Rope	Spin Class	Go Skating	Do Squats
Meat Less Monday	Tae Kwon Do	Do Zumba	Do Tai Chi	Kick Boxing
Ride a Bike	Water Fast	Less Carbs	Go Hiking	Do Cardio

EVENING RITUAL

I Will Maintain My Vibration By:

	Mon	Tues	Wed	Thurs	Fri
_____	○	○	○	○	○
_____	○	○	○	○	○
_____	○	○	○	○	○
_____	○	○	○	○	○
_____	○	○	○	○	○
_____	○	○	○	○	○

RITUAL SUGGESTIONS LOCATED ON THE RISING RITUALS PAGE

SLEEP CHECK

Getting enough sleep daily ensures you are well rested and ready to tackle the day. Try pushing for seven to eight hours of sleep a night

	SUN	MON	TUE	WED	THU	FRI	SAT
Go to sleep time							
Wake up time							
How long I slept							

WEEKLY REFLECTION

GOALS ACHIEVED:

HIGHLIGHTS:

GOALS FOR NEXT WEEK:

WEEKEND RESTORATION

ADD YOUR WEEKEND SELF CARE PLANS BELOW

-
-
-

WEEKLY GOALS

- ✗ ....
- ✗ ....
- ✗ ....
- ✗ ....
- ✗ ....
- ✗ ....
- ✗ ....

WEEK SPECIFIC BOUNDARIES

I AM _____
(INSERT AFFIRMATION ABOVE)

This week, I Will Challenge Myself To:	Mon	Tues	Weds	Thurs	Fri

Weekly Tasks

	MON	TUE	WED	THU	FRI

FOR THE WEEK OF:

RISING RITUAL

I Will Raise My Vibration By:

	Mon	Tues	Wed	Thurs	Fri
_____	○	○	○	○	○
_____	○	○	○	○	○
_____	○	○	○	○	○
_____	○	○	○	○	○
_____	○	○	○	○	○

RITUAL SUGGESTIONS

EARLY RISE/ EARLY SET	GO TECH FREE	PRIORITIZE BALANCE	RECITE YOUR AFFIRMATIONS	JOURNAL
GO FOR A WALK	MORNING/ EVENING DRINK	SET MILESTONES	BREATHWORK	VISUALIZE SUCCESS
READ	TAKE A HERBAL BATH	EXPRESS GRATITUDE	CLEAN UP	PAMPER YOURSELF
UNPLUG	REVIEW GOALS & TO-DO LISTS	WORK DELIBERATELY	SET INTENTIONS	EMBRACE NATURE
FEED YOUR MIND	EXERCISE	MEDITATE	GET ORGANIZED	LISTEN TO A PODCAST

DON'T OVER STRESS YOURSELF TO AVOID FATIGUE. IT'S NEARLY IMPOSSIBLE TO BE IN A POSITIVE MENTAL STATE WHEN YOUR BODY IS STRESSED OUT.

WEEKLY EXERCISE
THIS WEEK I CHOOSE TO...

- _____
- _____
- _____
- _____
- _____
- _____

WEEKLY FOOD DIARY
LESS OR MORE OF WHAT?

Breakfast:

Lunch:

Dinner:

Snacks:

Beverages:

FITNESS SUGGESTIONS

Do Yoga	Martial Arts	Go for a Walk	Take the Stairs	Eat Less Meat
No sugar	Go Swimming	Dance Party	Team Sports	Yard Work
Do Pilates	Jump Rope	Spin Class	Go Skating	Do Squats
Meat Less Monday	Tae Kwon Do	Do Zumba	Do Tai Chi	Kick Boxing
Ride a Bike	Water Fast	Less Carbs	Go Hiking	Do Cardio

EVENING RITUAL

I Will Maintain My Vibration By:	Mon	Tues	Wed	Thurs	Fri
_____	○	○	○	○	○
_____	○	○	○	○	○
_____	○	○	○	○	○
_____	○	○	○	○	○
_____	○	○	○	○	○
_____	○	○	○	○	○

RITUAL SUGGESTIONS LOCATED ON THE RISING RITUALS PAGE

SLEEP CHECK

Getting enough sleep daily ensures you are well rested and ready to tackle the day. Try pushing for seven to eight hours of sleep a night

	SUN	MON	TUE	WED	THU	FRI	SAT
Go to sleep time							
Wake up time							
How long I slept							

WEEKLY REFLECTION

_____
_____
_____

GOALS ACHIEVED:

HIGHLIGHTS:

GOALS FOR NEXT WEEK:

WEEKEND RESTORATION
ADD YOUR WEEKEND SELF CARE PLANS BELOW

END OF MONTH RECAP

SMALL WINS
1. _____
2. _____
3. _____

BIG ACHIEVEMENTS
1. _____
2. _____
3. _____

HIGHLIGHTS

LESSONS I LEARNED

WHAT WORKED

WHAT I'LL STOP DOING

IMPROVEMENTS TO MAKE

M	T	W	T	F	S	S

Top Priorities

_____
_____
_____
_____
_____
_____
_____
_____
_____

Notes

MONTHLY GOALS

MY FOCUS IS ON

MILESTONES
1.
2.
3.

DO   DON'T

MAIN GOALS
1.
2.
3.
4.
5.

IMPORTANT DATES

GOAL SUGGESTIONS

REACH OUT TO AN INFLUENCER	HEALTHY WORK/LIFE BALANCE	PRACTICE CONFIDENCE	EMAIL 10 NEW PROSPECTS ABOUT MY BUSINESS	LET GO OF LIMITING BELIEFS	IMPROVE CUSTOMER ENGAGEMENT
WORK ON MY SOCIAL MEDIA PRESENCE	PRACTICE DECISVENESS	LEARN A NEW SKILL	INCREASE SALES	PRACTICE MINDFULNESS	REDUCE BUSINESS EXPENSES
FIND NEW HOBBIES	WORK ON MY MARKETING STRATEGY	DELEGATE EFFECTIVELY	STAND UP TO MY FEARS	WORK WITH IDEAL CLIENTS	PLAN MY MARKETING CALENDAR

MONTHLY BUDGET

MONTH OF: _____

INCOME			
DATE	SOURCE	CATEGORY	AMOUNT

BILLS & FIXED EXPENSES		
DATE	SOURCE	AMOUNT

VARIABLE EXPENSES		
DATE	SOURCE	AMOUNT

SUMMARY	
SOURCE	AMOUNT
INCOME	
BILLS & FIXED EXPENSES	
VARIABLE EXPENSES	
BALANCE	

SOCIAL MEDIA POSTING SCHEDULE

Test out the three social media networks you chose to focus on

Month: _____ **Monthly Focus:** _____

NETWORK	SUN	MON	TUE	WED	THU	FRI	SAT

NETWORK	SUN	MON	TUE	WED	THU	FRI	SAT

NETWORK	SUN	MON	TUE	WED	THU	FRI	SAT

NETWORK	SUN	MON	TUE	WED	THU	FRI	SAT

PROGRESS TRACKER

KEY

START BY COLORING IN EACH BOX IN THE GRAY KEY AREA WITH A DIFFERENT COLOR. NEXT TO THE BOX, YOU WILL CREATE PERFORMANCE METRICS FOR THE MONTH.
FOR EX: PROJECTS COMPLETED, NEW CLIENTS, RETURNING CLIENTS, SOCIAL MEDIA GROWTH, SALES, WEBSITE SUBSCRIBERS, ETC.

WHENEVER YOU MAKE PROGRESS THIS MONTH TOWARDS ONE OF THESE GOALS, COME BACK AND FILL IN A PART OF THE WOLF WITH THE CORRESPONDING COLOR.

DAILY GRATITUDE LOG

WRITE DOWN 3 THINGS YOU ARE GRATEFUL FOR ON EACH LINE

1. ....
2. ....
3. ....
4. ....
5. ....
6. ....
7. ....
8. ....
9. ....
10. ....
11. ....
12. ....
13. ....
14. ....
15. ....
16. ....
17. ....
18. ....
19. ....
20. ....
21. ....
22. ....
23. ....
24. ....
25. ....
26. ....
27. ....
28. ....
29. ....
30. ....
31. ....

WEEKLY GOALS

- ✗ ....
- ✗ ....
- ✗ ....
- ✗ ....
- ✗ ....
- ✗ ....
- ✗ ....

WEEK SPECIFIC BOUNDARIES

I AM _____
(INSERT AFFIRMATION ABOVE)

This week, I Will Challenge Myself To:	Mon	Tues	Weds	Thurs	Fri

Weekly Tasks

MON TUE WED THU FRI

FOR THE
WEEK OF:

RISING RITUAL

I Will Raise My Vibration By:

	Mon	Tues	Wed	Thurs	Fri
_____	○	○	○	○	○
_____	○	○	○	○	○
_____	○	○	○	○	○
_____	○	○	○	○	○
_____	○	○	○	○	○

RITUAL SUGGESTIONS

EARLY RISE/ EARLY SET	GO TECH FREE	PRIORITIZE BALANCE	RECITE MY AFFIRMATIONS	JOURNAL
GO FOR A WALK	MORNING/ EVENING DRINK	SET MILESTONES	BREATHWORK	VISUALIZE SUCCESS
READ	TAKE A HERBAL BATH	EXPRESS GRATITUDE	CLEAN UP	PAMPER MYSELF
UNPLUG	REVIEW GOALS & TO-DO LISTS	WORK DELIBERATELY	SET INTENTIONS	EMBRACE NATURE
FEED MY MIND	EXERCISE	MEDITATE	GET ORGANIZED	LISTEN TO A PODCAST

DON'T OVER STRESS YOURSELF TO AVOID FATIGUE. IT'S NEARLY IMPOSSIBLE TO BE IN A POSITIVE MENTAL STATE WHEN YOUR BODY IS STRESSED OUT.

WEEKLY EXERCISE
THIS WEEK I CHOOSE TO...

- _____
- _____
- _____
- _____
- _____
- _____

WEEKLY FOOD DIARY
LESS OR MORE OF WHAT?

Breakfast:
_____

Lunch:
_____

Dinner:
_____

Snacks:
_____

Beverages:
_____

FITNESS SUGGESTIONS

Do Yoga	Martial Arts	Go for a Walk	Take the Stairs	Eat Less Meat
No sugar	Go Swimming	Dance Party	Team Sports	Yard Work
Do Pilates	Jump Rope	Spin Class	Go Skating	Do Squats
Meat Less Monday	Tae Kwon Do	Do Zumba	Do Tai Chi	Kick Boxing
Ride a Bike	Water Fast	Less Carbs	Go Hiking	Do Cardio

EVENING RITUAL

I Will Maintain My Vibration By:	Mon	Tues	Wed	Thurs	Fri
_____	○	○	○	○	○
_____	○	○	○	○	○
_____	○	○	○	○	○
_____	○	○	○	○	○
_____	○	○	○	○	○
_____	○	○	○	○	○

RITUAL SUGGESTIONS LOCATED ON THE RISING RITUALS PAGE

SLEEP CHECK

Getting enough sleep daily ensures you are well rested and ready to tackle the day. Try pushing for seven to eight hours of sleep a night

	SUN	MON	TUE	WED	THU	FRI	SAT
Go to sleep time							
Wake up time							
How long I slept							

WEEKLY REFLECTION

GOALS ACHIEVED:

HIGHLIGHTS:

GOALS FOR NEXT WEEK:

WEEKEND RESTORATION
ADD YOUR WEEKEND SELF CARE PLANS BELOW

WEEKLY GOALS

- ✗ ....
- ✗ ....
- ✗ ....
- ✗ ....
- ✗ ....
- ✗ ....
- ✗ ....

WEEK SPECIFIC BOUNDARIES

I AM _____
(INSERT AFFIRMATION ABOVE)

This week, I Will Challenge Myself To:	Mon	Tues	Weds	Thurs	Fri

Weekly Tasks

MON TUE WED THU FRI

FOR THE
WEEK OF:

RISING RITUAL

I Will Raise My Vibration By:

	Mon	Tues	Wed	Thurs	Fri
_____	○	○	○	○	○
_____	○	○	○	○	○
_____	○	○	○	○	○
_____	○	○	○	○	○
_____	○	○	○	○	○

RITUAL SUGGESTIONS

EARLY RISE/ EARLY SET	GO TECH FREE	PRIORITIZE BALANCE	RECITE YOUR AFFIRMATIONS	JOURNAL
GO FOR A WALK	MORNING/ EVENING DRINK	SET MILESTONES	BREATHWORK	VISUALIZE SUCCESS
READ	TAKE A HERBAL BATH	EXPRESS GRATITUDE	CLEAN UP	PAMPER YOURSELF
UNPLUG	REVIEW GOALS & TO-DO LISTS	WORK DELIBERATELY	SET INTENTIONS	EMBRACE NATURE
FEED YOUR MIND	EXERCISE	MEDITATE	GET ORGANIZED	LISTEN TO A PODCAST

DON'T OVER STRESS YOURSELF TO AVOID FATIGUE. IT'S NEARLY IMPOSSIBLE TO BE IN A POSITIVE MENTAL STATE WHEN YOUR BODY IS STRESSED OUT.

WEEKLY EXERCISE
THIS WEEK I CHOOSE TO...

- _____
- _____
- _____
- _____
- _____
- _____

WEEKLY FOOD DIARY
LESS OR MORE OF WHAT?

Breakfast: _____

Lunch: _____

Dinner: _____

Snacks: _____

Beverages: _____

FITNESS SUGGESTIONS

Do Yoga	Martial Arts	Go for a Walk	Take the Stairs	Eat Less Meat
No sugar	Go Swimming	Dance Party	Team Sports	Yard Work
Do Pilates	Jump Rope	Spin Class	Go Skating	Do Squats
Meat Less Monday	Tae Kwon Do	Do Zumba	Do Tai Chi	Kick Boxing
Ride a Bike	Water Fast	Less Carbs	Go Hiking	Do Cardio

EVENING RITUAL

I Will Maintain My Vibration By: Mon   Tues   Wed   Thurs   Fri

_____

_____

_____

_____

_____

_____

RITUAL SUGGESTIONS LOCATED ON THE RISING RITUALS PAGE

SLEEP CHECK

Getting enough sleep daily ensures you are well rested and ready to tackle the day. Try pushing for seven to eight hours of sleep a night

	SUN	MON	TUE	WED	THU	FRI	SAT
Go to sleep time							
Wake up time							
How long I slept							

WEEKLY REFLECTION

GOALS ACHIEVED:

HIGHLIGHTS:

GOALS FOR NEXT WEEK:

WEEKEND RESTORATION
ADD YOUR WEEKEND SELF CARE PLANS BELOW

WEEKLY GOALS

✗ ....
✗ ....
✗ ....
✗ ....
✗ ....
✗ ....
✗ ....

WEEK SPECIFIC BOUNDARIES

I AM _____
(INSERT AFFIRMATION ABOVE)

This week, I Will Challenge Myself To:

	Mon	Tues	Weds	Thurs	Fri

Weekly Tasks

MON TUE WED THU FRI

FOR THE
WEEK OF:

RISING RITUAL

I Will Raise My Vibration By: Mon   Tues   Wed   Thurs   Fri

_____

_____

_____

_____

_____

RITUAL SUGGESTIONS

EARLY RISE/ EARLY SET	GO TECH FREE	PRIORITIZE BALANCE	RECITE YOUR AFFIRMATIONS	JOURNAL
GO FOR A WALK	MORNING/ EVENING DRINK	SET MILESTONES	BREATHWORK	VISUALIZE SUCCESS
READ	TAKE A HERBAL BATH	EXPRESS GRATITUDE	CLEAN UP	PAMPER YOURSELF
UNPLUG	REVIEW GOALS & TO-DO LISTS	WORK DELIBERATELY	SET INTENTIONS	EMBRACE NATURE
FEED YOUR MIND	EXERCISE	MEDITATE	GET ORGANIZED	LISTEN TO A PODCAST

DON'T OVER STRESS YOURSELF TO AVOID FATIGUE. IT'S NEARLY IMPOSSIBLE TO BE IN A POSITIVE MENTAL STATE WHEN YOUR BODY IS STRESSED OUT.

WEEKLY EXERCISE
THIS WEEK I CHOOSE TO...

○ _____

○ _____

○ _____

○ _____

○ _____

○ _____

WEEKLY FOOD DIARY
LESS OR MORE OF WHAT?

Breakfast:
_____

Lunch:
_____

Dinner:
_____

Snacks:
_____

Beverages:
_____

FITNESS SUGGESTIONS

Do Yoga	Martial Arts	Go for a Walk	Take the Stairs	Eat Less Meat
No sugar	Go Swimming	Dance Party	Team Sports	Yard Work
Do Pilates	Jump Rope	Spin Class	Go Skating	Do Squats
Meat Less Monday	Tae Kwon Do	Do Zumba	Do Tai Chi	Kick Boxing
Ride a Bike	Water Fast	Less Carbs	Go Hiking	Do Cardio

EVENING RITUAL

I Will Maintain My Vibration By: Mon   Tues   Wed   Thurs   Fri

_____

_____

_____

_____

_____

_____

RITUAL SUGGESTIONS LOCATED ON THE RISING RITUALS PAGE

SLEEP CHECK

Getting enough sleep daily ensures you are well rested and ready to tackle the day. Try pushing for seven to eight hours of sleep a night

	SUN	MON	TUE	WED	THU	FRI	SAT
Go to sleep time							
Wake up time							
How long I slept							

WEEKLY REFLECTION

GOALS ACHIEVED:

HIGHLIGHTS:

GOALS FOR NEXT WEEK:

WEEKEND RESTORATION

ADD YOUR WEEKEND SELF CARE PLANS BELOW

WEEKLY GOALS

✗ ....
✗ ....
✗ ....
✗ ....
✗ ....
✗ ....
✗ ....

WEEK SPECIFIC BOUNDARIES

I AM _____
(INSERT AFFIRMATION ABOVE)

This week, I Will Challenge Myself To:	Mon	Tues	Weds	Thurs	Fri

Weekly Tasks

	MON	TUE	WED	THU	FRI

FOR THE WEEK OF:

RISING RITUAL

I Will Raise My Vibration By:

	Mon	Tues	Wed	Thurs	Fri
_____	○	○	○	○	○
_____	○	○	○	○	○
_____	○	○	○	○	○
_____	○	○	○	○	○
_____	○	○	○	○	○

RITUAL SUGGESTIONS

EARLY RISE/ EARLY SET	GO TECH FREE	PRIORITIZE BALANCE	RECITE YOUR AFFIRMATIONS	JOURNAL
GO FOR A WALK	MORNING/ EVENING DRINK	SET MILESTONES	BREATHWORK	VISUALIZE SUCCESS
READ	TAKE A HERBAL BATH	EXPRESS GRATITUDE	CLEAN UP	PAMPER YOURSELF
UNPLUG	REVIEW GOALS & TO-DO LISTS	WORK DELIBERATELY	SET INTENTIONS	EMBRACE NATURE
FEED YOUR MIND	EXERCISE	MEDITATE	GET ORGANIZED	LISTEN TO A PODCAST

DON'T OVER STRESS YOURSELF TO AVOID FATIGUE. IT'S NEARLY IMPOSSIBLE TO BE IN A POSITIVE MENTAL STATE WHEN YOUR BODY IS STRESSED OUT.

WEEKLY EXERCISE
THIS WEEK I CHOOSE TO...

- _____
- _____
- _____
- _____
- _____
- _____

WEEKLY FOOD DIARY
LESS OR MORE OF WHAT?

Breakfast:

Lunch:

Dinner:

Snacks:

Beverages:

FITNESS SUGGESTIONS

Do Yoga	Martial Arts	Go for a Walk	Take the Stairs	Eat Less Meat
No sugar	Go Swimming	Dance Party	Team Sports	Yard Work
Do Pilates	Jump Rope	Spin Class	Go Skating	Do Squats
Meat Less Monday	Tae Kwon Do	Do Zumba	Do Tai Chi	Kick Boxing
Ride a Bike	Water Fast	Less Carbs	Go Hiking	Do Cardio

EVENING RITUAL

I Will Maintain My Vibration By:

	Mon	Tues	Wed	Thurs	Fri
_____	○	○	○	○	○
_____	○	○	○	○	○
_____	○	○	○	○	○
_____	○	○	○	○	○
_____	○	○	○	○	○
_____	○	○	○	○	○

RITUAL SUGGESTIONS LOCATED ON THE RISING RITUALS PAGE

SLEEP CHECK

Getting enough sleep daily ensures you are well rested and ready to tackle the day. Try pushing for seven to eight hours of sleep a night

	SUN	MON	TUE	WED	THU	FRI	SAT
Go to sleep time							
Wake up time							
How long I slept							

WEEKLY REFLECTION

GOALS ACHIEVED:

HIGHLIGHTS:

GOALS FOR NEXT WEEK:

WEEKEND RESTORATION

ADD YOUR WEEKEND SELF CARE PLANS BELOW

END OF MONTH RECAP

SMALL WINS
1. _____
2. _____
3. _____

BIG ACHIEVEMENTS
1. _____
2. _____
3. _____

HIGHLIGHTS

LESSONS I LEARNED

WHAT WORKED

WHAT I'LL STOP DOING

IMPROVEMENTS TO MAKE

M	T	W	T	F	S	S

Top Priorities

_____
_____
_____
_____
_____
_____
_____
_____
_____

Notes

MONTHLY GOALS

MY FOCUS IS ON

MILESTONES
1
2
3

DO   DON'T

MAIN GOALS
1
2
3
4
5

IMPORTANT DATES

GOAL SUGGESTIONS

REACH OUT TO AN INFLUENCER	HEALTHY WORK/LIFE BALANCE	PRACTICE CONFIDENCE	EMAIL 10 NEW PROSPECTS ABOUT MY BUSINESS	LET GO OF LIMITING BELIEFS	IMPROVE CUSTOMER ENGAGEMENT	
WORK ON MY SOCIAL MEDIA PRESENCE	PRACTICE DECISVENESS	LEARN A NEW SKILL	INCREASE SALES	PRACTICE MINDFULNESS	REDUCE BUSINESS EXPENSES	
FIND NEW HOBBIES	WORK ON MY MARKETING STRATEGY	DELEGATE EFFECTIVELY	STAND UP TO MY FEARS	WORK WITH IDEAL CLIENTS	PLAN MY MARKETING CALENDAR	

MONTHLY BUDGET

MONTH OF: _____

INCOME			
DATE	SOURCE	CATEGORY	AMOUNT

BILLS & FIXED EXPENSES		
DATE	SOURCE	AMOUNT

VARIABLE EXPENSES		
DATE	SOURCE	AMOUNT

SUMMARY	
SOURCE	AMOUNT
INCOME	
BILLS & FIXED EXPENSES	
VARIABLE EXPENSES	
BALANCE	

SOCIAL MEDIA POSTING SCHEDULE

Test out the three social media networks you chose to focus on

Month: _____ **Monthly Focus:** _____

NETWORK	SUN	MON	TUE	WED	THU	FRI	SAT

NETWORK	SUN	MON	TUE	WED	THU	FRI	SAT

NETWORK	SUN	MON	TUE	WED	THU	FRI	SAT

NETWORK	SUN	MON	TUE	WED	THU	FRI	SAT

PROGRESS TRACKER

START BY COLORING IN EACH BOX IN THE GRAY KEY AREA WITH A DIFFERENT COLOR. NEXT TO THE BOX, YOU WILL CREATE PERFORMANCE METRICS FOR THE MONTH.
FOR EX: PROJECTS COMPLETED, NEW CLIENTS, RETURNING CLIENTS, SOCIAL MEDIA GROWTH, SALES, WEBSITE SUBSCRIBERS, ETC.

WHENEVER YOU MAKE PROGRESS THIS MONTH TOWARDS ONE OF THESE GOALS, COME BACK AND FILL IN A PART OF THE WOLF WITH THE CORRESPONDING COLOR.

KEY

DAILY GRATITUDE LOG

WRITE DOWN 3 THINGS YOU ARE GRATEFUL FOR ON EACH LINE

1. ....
2. ....
3. ....
4. ....
5. ....
6. ....
7. ....
8. ....
9. ....
10. ....
11. ....
12. ....
13. ....
14. ....
15. ....
16. ....
17. ....
18. ....
19. ....
20. ....
21. ....
22. ....
23. ....
24. ....
25. ....
26. ....
27. ....
28. ....
29. ....
30. ....
31. ....

WEEKLY GOALS

- ✗ ....
- ✗ ....
- ✗ ....
- ✗ ....
- ✗ ....
- ✗ ....
- ✗ ....

WEEK SPECIFIC BOUNDARIES

I AM _____
(INSERT AFFIRMATION ABOVE)

This week, I Will Challenge Myself To:

	Mon	Tues	Weds	Thurs	Fri

Weekly Tasks

MON TUE WED THU FRI

FOR THE
WEEK OF:

RISING RITUAL

I Will Raise My Vibration By:

	Mon	Tues	Wed	Thurs	Fri
_____	○	○	○	○	○
_____	○	○	○	○	○
_____	○	○	○	○	○
_____	○	○	○	○	○
_____	○	○	○	○	○

RITUAL SUGGESTIONS

EARLY RISE/ EARLY SET	GO TECH FREE	PRIORITIZE BALANCE	RECITE MY AFFIRMATIONS	JOURNAL
GO FOR A WALK	MORNING/ EVENING DRINK	SET MILESTONES	BREATHWORK	VISUALIZE SUCCESS
READ	TAKE A HERBAL BATH	EXPRESS GRATITUDE	CLEAN UP	PAMPER MYSELF
UNPLUG	REVIEW GOALS & TO-DO LISTS	WORK DELIBERATELY	SET INTENTIONS	EMBRACE NATURE
FEED MY MIND	EXERCISE	MEDITATE	GET ORGANIZED	LISTEN TO A PODCAST

DON'T OVER STRESS YOURSELF TO AVOID FATIGUE. IT'S NEARLY IMPOSSIBLE TO BE IN A POSITIVE MENTAL STATE WHEN YOUR BODY IS STRESSED OUT.

WEEKLY EXERCISE
THIS WEEK I CHOOSE TO...

- _____
- _____
- _____
- _____
- _____
- _____

WEEKLY FOOD DIARY
LESS OR MORE OF WHAT?

Breakfast:

Lunch:

Dinner:

Snacks:

Beverages:

FITNESS SUGGESTIONS

Do Yoga	Martial Arts	Go for a Walk	Take the Stairs	Eat Less Meat
No sugar	Go Swimming	Dance Party	Team Sports	Yard Work
Do Pilates	Jump Rope	Spin Class	Go Skating	Do Squats
Meat Less Monday	Tae Kwon Do	Do Zumba	Do Tai Chi	Kick Boxing
Ride a Bike	Water Fast	Less Carbs	Go Hiking	Do Cardio

EVENING RITUAL

I Will Maintain My Vibration By:	Mon	Tues	Wed	Thurs	Fri
_____	○	○	○	○	○
_____	○	○	○	○	○
_____	○	○	○	○	○
_____	○	○	○	○	○
_____	○	○	○	○	○
_____	○	○	○	○	○

RITUAL SUGGESTIONS LOCATED ON THE RISING RITUALS PAGE

SLEEP CHECK

Getting enough sleep daily ensures you are well rested and ready to tackle the day. Try pushing for seven to eight hours of sleep a night

	SUN	MON	TUE	WED	THU	FRI	SAT
Go to sleep time							
Wake up time							
How long I slept							

WEEKLY REFLECTION

GOALS ACHIEVED:

HIGHLIGHTS:

GOALS FOR NEXT WEEK:

WEEKEND RESTORATION

ADD YOUR WEEKEND SELF CARE PLANS BELOW

WEEKLY GOALS

- ✗ ....
- ✗ ....
- ✗ ....
- ✗ ....
- ✗ ....
- ✗ ....

WEEK SPECIFIC BOUNDARIES

I AM _____
(INSERT AFFIRMATION ABOVE)

This week, I Will Challenge Myself To:

	Mon	Tues	Weds	Thurs	Fri

Weekly Tasks

MON TUE WED THU FRI

FOR THE
WEEK OF:

RISING RITUAL

I Will Raise My Vibration By: Mon   Tues   Wed   Thurs   Fri

_____

_____

_____

_____

_____

RITUAL SUGGESTIONS

EARLY RISE/ EARLY SET	GO TECH FREE	PRIORITIZE BALANCE	RECITE YOUR AFFIRMATIONS	JOURNAL
GO FOR A WALK	MORNING/ EVENING DRINK	SET MILESTONES	BREATHWORK	VISUALIZE SUCCESS
READ	TAKE A HERBAL BATH	EXPRESS GRATITUDE	CLEAN UP	PAMPER YOURSELF
UNPLUG	REVIEW GOALS & TO-DO LISTS	WORK DELIBERATELY	SET INTENTIONS	EMBRACE NATURE
FEED YOUR MIND	EXERCISE	MEDITATE	GET ORGANIZED	LISTEN TO A PODCAST

DON'T OVER STRESS YOURSELF TO AVOID FATIGUE. IT'S NEARLY IMPOSSIBLE TO BE IN A POSITIVE MENTAL STATE WHEN YOUR BODY IS STRESSED OUT.

WEEKLY EXERCISE
THIS WEEK I CHOOSE TO...

- _____
- _____
- _____
- _____
- _____
- _____

WEEKLY FOOD DIARY
LESS OR MORE OF WHAT?

Breakfast:

Lunch:

Dinner:

Snacks:

Beverages:

FITNESS SUGGESTIONS

Do Yoga	Martial Arts	Go for a Walk	Take the Stairs	Eat Less Meat
No sugar	Go Swimming	Dance Party	Team Sports	Yard Work
Do Pilates	Jump Rope	Spin Class	Go Skating	Do Squats
Meat Less Monday	Tae Kwon Do	Do Zumba	Do Tai Chi	Kick Boxing
Ride a Bike	Water Fast	Less Carbs	Go Hiking	Do Cardio

EVENING RITUAL

I Will Maintain My Vibration By: Mon   Tues   Wed   Thurs   Fri

_____

_____

_____

_____

_____

RITUAL SUGGESTIONS LOCATED ON THE RISING RITUALS PAGE

SLEEP CHECK

Getting enough sleep daily ensures you are well rested and ready to tackle the day. Try pushing for seven to eight hours of sleep a night

	SUN	MON	TUE	WED	THU	FRI	SAT
Go to sleep time							
Wake up time							
How long I slept							

WEEKLY REFLECTION

_____
_____
_____
_____

GOALS ACHIEVED:

HIGHLIGHTS:

GOALS FOR NEXT WEEK:

WEEKEND RESTORATION

ADD YOUR WEEKEND SELF CARE PLANS BELOW

WEEKLY GOALS

- ✗ ....
- ✗ ....
- ✗ ....
- ✗ ....
- ✗ ....
- ✗ ....
- ✗ ....

WEEK SPECIFIC BOUNDARIES

I AM _____
(INSERT AFFIRMATION ABOVE)

This week, I Will Challenge Myself To:

	Mon	Tues	Weds	Thurs	Fri

Weekly Tasks

FOR THE
WEEK OF:

	MON	TUE	WED	THU	FRI

RISING RITUAL

I Will Raise My Vibration By:

	Mon	Tues	Wed	Thurs	Fri
_____	○	○	○	○	○
_____	○	○	○	○	○
_____	○	○	○	○	○
_____	○	○	○	○	○
_____	○	○	○	○	○

RITUAL SUGGESTIONS

EARLY RISE/ EARLY SET	GO TECH FREE	PRIORITIZE BALANCE	RECITE YOUR AFFIRMATIONS	JOURNAL
GO FOR A WALK	MORNING/ EVENING DRINK	SET MILESTONES	BREATHWORK	VISUALIZE SUCCESS
READ	TAKE A HERBAL BATH	EXPRESS GRATITUDE	CLEAN UP	PAMPER YOURSELF
UNPLUG	REVIEW GOALS & TO-DO LISTS	WORK DELIBERATELY	SET INTENTIONS	EMBRACE NATURE
FEED YOUR MIND	EXERCISE	MEDITATE	GET ORGANIZED	LISTEN TO A PODCAST

DON'T OVER STRESS YOURSELF TO AVOID FATIGUE. IT'S NEARLY IMPOSSIBLE TO BE IN A POSITIVE MENTAL STATE WHEN YOUR BODY IS STRESSED OUT.

WEEKLY EXERCISE
THIS WEEK I CHOOSE TO...

- _____
- _____
- _____
- _____
- _____
- _____

WEEKLY FOOD DIARY
LESS OR MORE OF WHAT?

Breakfast:
_____

Lunch:
_____

Dinner:
_____

Snacks:
_____

Beverages:
_____

FITNESS SUGGESTIONS

Do Yoga	Martial Arts	Go for a Walk	Take the Stairs	Eat Less Meat
No sugar	Go Swimming	Dance Party	Team Sports	Yard Work
Do Pilates	Jump Rope	Spin Class	Go Skating	Do Squats
Meat Less Monday	Tae Kwon Do	Do Zumba	Do Tai Chi	Kick Boxing
Ride a Bike	Water Fast	Less Carbs	Go Hiking	Do Cardio

EVENING RITUAL

I Will Maintain My Vibration By: Mon Tues Wed Thurs Fri

_____

_____

_____

_____

_____

RITUAL SUGGESTIONS LOCATED ON THE RISING RITUALS PAGE

SLEEP CHECK

Getting enough sleep daily ensures you are well rested and ready to tackle the day. Try pushing for seven to eight hours of sleep a night

	SUN	MON	TUE	WED	THU	FRI	SAT
Go to sleep time							
Wake up time							
How long I slept							

WEEKLY REFLECTION

GOALS ACHIEVED:

HIGHLIGHTS:

GOALS FOR NEXT WEEK:

WEEKEND RESTORATION

ADD YOUR WEEKEND SELF CARE PLANS BELOW

-
-
-

WEEKLY GOALS

- ✗ ....
- ✗ ....
- ✗ ....
- ✗ ....
- ✗ ....
- ✗ ....
- ✗ ....

WEEK SPECIFIC BOUNDARIES

I AM _____
(INSERT AFFIRMATION ABOVE)

This week, I Will Challenge Myself To:

	Mon	Tues	Weds	Thurs	Fri

Weekly Tasks

	MON	TUE	WED	THU	FRI

FOR THE
WEEK OF:

RISING RITUAL

I Will Raise My Vibration By: Mon   Tues   Wed   Thurs   Fri

_____

_____

_____

_____

_____

RITUAL SUGGESTIONS

EARLY RISE/ EARLY SET	GO TECH FREE	PRIORITIZE BALANCE	RECITE YOUR AFFIRMATIONS	JOURNAL
GO FOR A WALK	MORNING/ EVENING DRINK	SET MILESTONES	BREATHWORK	VISUALIZE SUCCESS
READ	TAKE A HERBAL BATH	EXPRESS GRATITUDE	CLEAN UP	PAMPER YOURSELF
UNPLUG	REVIEW GOALS & TO-DO LISTS	WORK DELIBERATELY	SET INTENTIONS	EMBRACE NATURE
FEED YOUR MIND	EXERCISE	MEDITATE	GET ORGANIZED	LISTEN TO A PODCAST

DON'T OVER STRESS YOURSELF TO AVOID FATIGUE. IT'S NEARLY IMPOSSIBLE TO BE IN A POSITIVE MENTAL STATE WHEN YOUR BODY IS STRESSED OUT.

WEEKLY EXERCISE
THIS WEEK I CHOOSE TO...

- _____
- _____
- _____
- _____
- _____
- _____

WEEKLY FOOD DIARY
LESS OR MORE OF WHAT?

Breakfast:

Lunch:

Dinner:

Snacks:

Beverages:

FITNESS SUGGESTIONS

Do Yoga	Martial Arts	Go for a Walk	Take the Stairs	Eat Less Meat
No sugar	Go Swimming	Dance Party	Team Sports	Yard Work
Do Pilates	Jump Rope	Spin Class	Go Skating	Do Squats
Meat Less Monday	Tae Kwon Do	Do Zumba	Do Tai Chi	Kick Boxing
Ride a Bike	Water Fast	Less Carbs	Go Hiking	Do Cardio

EVENING RITUAL

I Will Maintain My Vibration By: Mon   Tues   Wed   Thurs   Fri

_____

_____

_____

_____

_____

RITUAL SUGGESTIONS LOCATED ON THE RISING RITUALS PAGE

SLEEP CHECK

Getting enough sleep daily ensures you are well rested and ready to tackle the day. Try pushing for seven to eight hours of sleep a night

	SUN	MON	TUE	WED	THU	FRI	SAT
Go to sleep time							
Wake up time							
How long I slept							

WEEKLY REFLECTION

GOALS ACHIEVED:

HIGHLIGHTS:

GOALS FOR NEXT WEEK:

WEEKEND RESTORATION
ADD YOUR WEEKEND SELF CARE PLANS BELOW

-
-
-

END OF MONTH RECAP

SMALL WINS
1. _____
2. _____
3. _____

BIG ACHIEVEMENTS
1. _____
2. _____
3. _____

HIGHLIGHTS

LESSONS I LEARNED

WHAT WORKED

WHAT I'LL STOP DOING

IMPROVEMENTS TO MAKE

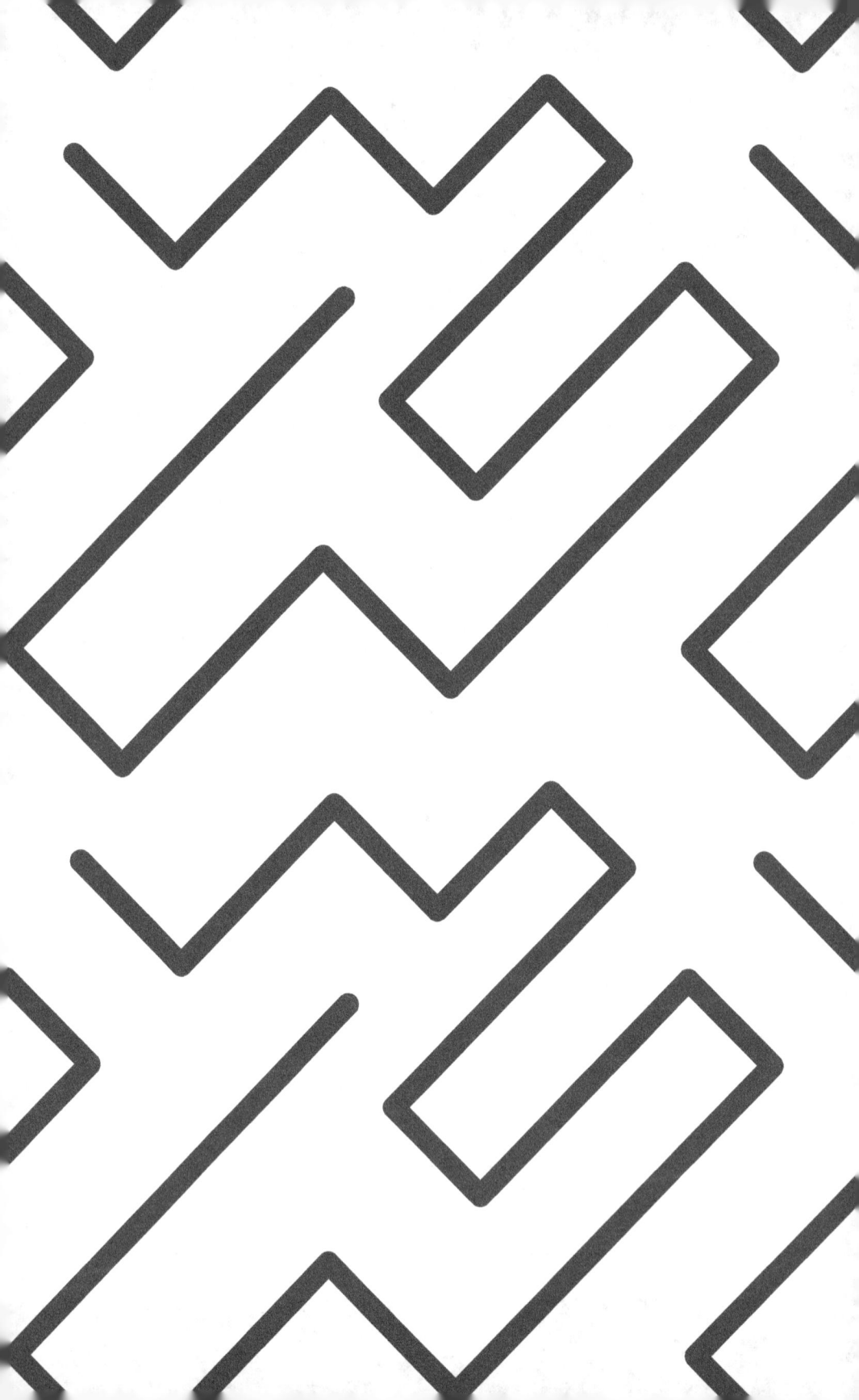

PASSWORD TRACKER

🌐 **Website -**
👤 **Username -**　　　　　　　　✏️ **Notes -**
🔑 **Password -**

🌐 **Website -**
👤 **Username -**　　　　　　　　✏️ **Notes -**
🔑 **Password -**

🌐 **Website -**
👤 **Username -**　　　　　　　　✏️ **Notes -**
🔑 **Password -**

🌐 **Website -**
👤 **Username -**　　　　　　　　✏️ **Notes -**
🔑 **Password -**

🌐 **Website -**
👤 **Username -**　　　　　　　　✏️ **Notes -**
🔑 **Password -**

🌐 **Website -**
👤 **Username -**　　　　　　　　✏️ **Notes -**
🔑 **Password -**

🌐 **Website -**
👤 **Username -**　　　　　　　　✏️ **Notes -**
🔑 **Password -**

🌐 **Website -**
👤 **Username -**　　　　　　　　✏️ **Notes -**
🔑 **Password -**

🌐 **Website -**
👤 **Username -**　　　　　　　　✏️ **Notes -**
🔑 **Password -**

🌐 **Website -**
👤 **Username -**　　　　　　　　✏️ **Notes -**
🔑 **Password -**

START UP COSTS

Keep track of your start up costs

Budget:

Item Description	Number of items	Cost	Date Purchased

Refer back to this page when filing your business taxes

PROFIT TRACKER

Month	Sales	Expenses	Profit	After Taxes

What I learned:

What I'll improve on the next six months:

ABOUT CREATOR

JASHAW

Brand Creator, Mentor,
& All Around Extraordinaire.

My mission is to help entrepreneurs develop the mindset needed to create a brand fueled by their passions in life, maintain good customer service, and ultimately be successful.

Facebook & Instagram:
@JAShawPro

Website:
JAShaw.org

ENTREPRENEUR'S MINDSET MENTOR PROGRAM

WITH BRAND CREATOR & MENTOR JASHAWPRO

- ✓ ENTREPRENEURIAL STRATEGY SESSIONS
- ✓ PATREON-ONLY UPDATES
- ✓ ENTREPRENEUR'S MINDSET CHAT COMMUNITY
- ✓ && SO MUCH MORE

Register Now — patreon.com/JAShawPro

GROW YOUR BRAND WITH JASHAWPRO

CONTENT CREATION

- ✓ GRAPHIC DESIGN & LOGOS
- ✓ WEBSITES & MAINTENANCE
- ✓ LANDING PAGES/FUNNELS
- ✓ CONTENT WRITING
- ✓ EMAIL MARKETING

CREATION EXTENSIONS

- ✓ ONLINE COURSE CREATION
- ✓ BOOK FORMATTING & PUBLISHING
- ✓ JOURNAL/PLANNER CREATION & PUBLISHING
- ✓ E BOOK CREATION & PUBLISHING
- ✓ GRAPHIC DESIGN & LOGOS

BRAND STRATEGIES

- ✓ START UP
- ✓ BRAND AWARENESS
- ✓ SOCIAL MEDIA
- ✓ EMAIL MARKETING
- ✓ BRAND EXPANSION & MENTORING

Publication Creation

If you are looking to publish a book, journal, piece of music, or other work for public sale- please send over an inquiry on your project to get started.

- Concept Consulting
- Ghost Writing
- ISBN purchase
- Copyright
- Book Cover Creation
- Publishing
- Website Design
- Printing and Distribution
- & More

You can schedule a discovery call by scanning this code

Consulting

Need assistance getting your project from point A to point B? Consulting rate $50 an hour, submit an inquiry today!

Production

Need assistance in the Creation, Design, & Production of your intended work? Submit an inquiry today!

Marketing

Need assistance with Branding, Website Design, Graphic Design, Social Media Marketing, E Marketing, & more Submit an inquiry today!

JAShaw.org
Email: JAShawPro@gmail.com

www.ingramcontent.com/pod-product-compliance
Lightning Source LLC
Chambersburg PA
CBHW070652120526
44590CB00013BA/925